Loving
THROUGH YOUR
Differences

Also by James L. Creighton

*CyberMeeting: How to Link People and Technology
in Your Organization* (with James W. R. Adams)

Don't Go Away Mad: How to Make Peace with Your Partner

Getting Well Again
(with O. Carl Simonton and Stephanie Matthews-Simonton)

*How Loving Couples Fight: 12 Essential Tools
for Working Through the Hurt*

Involving Citizens in Community Decision Making

The Public Involvement Handbook

The Public Participation Handbook

Loving
THROUGH YOUR
Differences

BUILDING STRONG RELATIONSHIPS
FROM SEPARATE REALITIES

JAMES L. CREIGHTON, PhD

New World Library
Novato, California

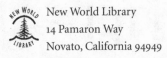

New World Library
14 Pamaron Way
Novato, California 94949

Text design by Tona Pearce Myers

Library of Congress Cataloging-in-Publication data is available.

First printing, February 2019
ISBN 978-1-60868-566-0
Ebook ISBN 978-1-60868-567-7
Printed in Canada on 100% postconsumer-waste recycled paper

New World Library is proud to be a Gold Certified Environmentally Responsible Publisher. Publisher certification awarded by Green Press Initiative. www.greenpressinitiative.org

10   9   8   7   6   5   4   3   2   1

To Florence Creighton,
a wise therapist of many years' experience,
who provided valuable help at every step of this book

Contents

Part 3: TOOLS AND APPROACHES

PART ONE

OUR ROLE
in
CREATING REALITY

CHAPTER ONE

Whose Reality Is Right?

Couples fight. Sometimes a little, sometimes a lot. Sometimes these fights provide comic relief. At other times they threaten the very survival of the relationship.

This is a book for people who fear conflicts with loved ones, or who are tired of hurting. The ideas and skills in this book have been field-tested: my wife and I just celebrated our fifty-second wedding anniversary. And our relationship hasn't always been easy. We certainly wouldn't have made it without the ideas and practices described in this book. We've learned by doing.

It has been my privilege to teach problem-solving and communication skills to thousands of people worldwide. Many of the people I've worked with have known not only the pain of fights but also additional challenges such as cancer, AIDS, domestic violence, probation, and even prison time.

One of the most important things I've learned is that each of us has an emotional reality of our own. No one else experiences events in the same way that you do. No one else has the same experiences of gender, childhood, religion, culture, and community that have shaped you. No one else has exactly the same beliefs, values, or philosophy of life.

This individuality means that two people may have entirely different emotional reactions to the same external event. If my wife and I go to a movie, I may find it exciting, while she is bored to tears. Whether or not the movie is any good is debatable — that's not fact. But it is a fact that I was excited. It is a fact that she felt bored.

We've all observed how people may react differently to the same event. Although it appears commonplace, this observation holds the key to a fundamentally different understanding of our feelings.

Most of us think of feelings as caused by events outside ourselves. We think we feel the way we do because of what other people do, or life events outside our control. We get in fights with our partner because of the things they say or do. If they would just be different, we'd feel good. If they would just stop doing the thing that's bothering us, we'd be okay. Or if they'd just start doing this other thing, we'd be okay. But in the meantime, there are moments when we are just miserable — and we think it's because of other people. When we think in this way, we are, in effect, giving away control over our feelings. We believe that in order for us to feel happy, other people must change what they are doing.

Our feelings are always filtered through and interpreted by our attitudes, beliefs, thoughts, expectations, and past history. This process creates our emotional reality.

If someone I know walks by me and pays no attention to me, I can interpret this behavior in several different ways:

- I can think he doesn't like me, or is upset with me, and is snubbing me intentionally.
- I can think that he has so much going on in his mind that paying attention to me is of secondary importance.
- I can think that he just didn't notice me.

Depending on my interpretation, I may feel hurt, angry, rejected, ignored, or just plain puzzled. My feeling results as much from my interpretation as from the other person's behavior.

We participate in creating our feelings by assigning meaning that we give to outside events. I'm not suggesting that we can simply sit down and decide what we're going to feel — although sometimes when we don't have all the facts or the situation is ambiguous, that's exactly what we do. Most of the time, our emotional reactions are instantaneous: someone says something, and we instantly feel upset, hurt, or rejected. We can feel those feelings in our body. But they are not caused directly by the event: they are the result of the interaction between the event and our personal emotional reality. It just happens so fast we're not aware of it.

How can we tell that this interaction is happening? We can see that other people feel differently about the same event. We may feel devastated by an event that other people think is no big deal. It is a fact that we feel devastated. It is a fact that these other people seem not to be bothered at all.

If we have a little emotional distance, it can be amusing when someone tells us that we ought to feel hurt, or rejected, or resentful about something that has happened, but we don't. They are really saying that because they would feel hurt (or rejected, or resentful) if that event happened to them, we should feel that way too.

Because their emotional reality is different, other people — including people we love, like our partners — have different emotional reactions to things than we do. We run into trouble when we expect — or even sometimes demand — that other people have the same perceptions that we do, and we are disappointed in them if they don't.

The problem comes when we blame these differences on

defects in their personality, moral sense, or compassion. In fact, in close relationships we often express this view by saying, "If you loved me, you would feel differently." We are essentially saying, "My emotional reality is the correct one. If you loved me, you would share my emotional reality."

The realization that the person we love doesn't share our emotional reality can be a source of great anxiety and alienation. We may ask ourselves, "What is this person doing in my life? We live in totally different worlds. We interpret everything differently. We don't like the same things. It is hard to imagine how we ever got together. Is it really possible to live with a person so unlike me, whose sense of reality doesn't even resemble my own?" We seem faced with a choice between being close to another person and standing alone with our own experience. Do we have to give up our own sense of the world, our own separate experience of reality, to be in relationship with another person?

This collision between separate realities is inevitable because it is rooted in the very nature of human perception. There comes a time, even in the most harmonious relationships, when we discover that hidden beneath those qualities that initially attracted us to the other person, there are differences that set us apart. We may have fundamentally different ideas about how to raise kids, spend money, or handle relationships with friends or relatives. We may have fundamentally different reactions to physical closeness or sexuality.

At times it may seem that we are living in two completely separate worlds, that the other person is unknown to us. We react differently to the same stimuli, situations, or experience. We interpret the same issues differently, and we have a different sense of what's right and proper. When, inevitably, this leads to conflict, we come face to face with the issue at the center of almost every human relationship: how to share our lives even though we sometimes experience separate realities.

The goal of this book is to help reduce conflicts between couples, especially conflicts based on different perceptions of reality. For example, what do you do when your partner is fearful of a possible outcome that you think is totally unlikely? How do you handle the fact that your partner is very threatened by an event that you thought was unimportant? What if the two of you have very different philosophies of child-rearing, or you just can't seem to come to agreement on how to manage money?

There are five common paths that couples tend to take following the discovery of their differences. (1) They begin a never-ending battle about who's right; both are hurt and angry and the fight continues. (2) One person gives up their own reality and does their best to adopt their partner's, often at the expense of real closeness. (3) One or both individuals decide to end the relationship, because it just seems like too much work. (4) One or both partners withdraw emotionally, minimizing all forms of communication between them, but still feel hurt or angry. (5) The couple makes a decision to discover the secrets of living happily and productively together, finding excitement and fulfillment, rather than disappointment and frustration, in their differences.

This book aims to provide you with the knowledge and practical skills to follow the fifth path. It will help you learn to see the differences in your perceptions and to use them as a way of gaining deeper understanding in order to develop relationships that are harmonious, exciting, and fulfilling.

Love alone is seldom enough to resolve differences. It is the skills we learn along the way — either through long, arduous trial and error, or more quickly and easily through books, workshops, and the help of counselors — that enable us to choose joy rather than grief.

There are many approaches to resolving conflicts based on different perceptions of reality. In this book I've tried to lay out a series of different ways to address your issues. The solution is likely to involve a combination of the approaches I present.

In part 1 I present a new way of thinking about reality, showing how we each interact differently with the outside world to create our unique emotional reality. This premise is central to the book.

At the end of part 1 I lay out eleven guidelines that I've found are essential to bridging differences. Subsequent chapters of the book elaborate upon these guidelines and provide specific skills and approaches for applying them.

The first set of guidelines, covered in part 2, addresses communication and problem-solving. Resolving a major conflict over differing realities can be challenging and may lead to hurtful arguments. The skills described in chapters 6–9 reduce the potential for conflict and can reduce the pain of any conflicts that do arise.

It's much easier to resolve conflicts if both people have learned to express feelings with minimal blame and accusation (chapter 6). You need to be able to listen with empathy to cross the divides that result from differing realities (chapter 7). When you see yourselves engaging in behaviors that make fights escalate, you can stop those behaviors (chapter 8). Collaborative problem-solving is a process for reaching agreements when there are still differences (chapter 9).

These skills can smooth the way toward resolving major differences. They may even be enough by themselves to resolve differences.

Part 3 describes paths of discovery couples can take together to find new ways of interpreting life's events and ultimately finding a shared understanding. Each path coincides with one of the fundamental guidelines. You may find yourself preferring one approach over another. That's fine. Go with what gives you energy and excitement.

Chapter 10 begins with the questions of values. The most difficult choices in life are rarely between good and bad: those decisions are usually not hard to make. The tough choices are between two things that are both good. We want security, but we also want freedom. We want creativity, but we also want discipline. These pairs of goods are often in tension with each other. Values choices entail assigning more weight or priority to one or the other.

Chapter 11 discusses a technique called reframing. Our feelings are shaped by the context or "frame" through which we perceive an experience or event. For example, behaviors that seem friendly in one context may seem overly familiar in another. Your partner may frame a situation differently than you do. Sometimes changing the frame makes it possible to find solutions that are acceptable to both people.

Chapter 12 addresses the biggest frame of all, our life stories. We've learned to view our lives within a frame that shapes our behavior: for example, we may tell ourselves, "I'm a shy person," or "I'm a survivor." Some people view their lives as failures, and everything that happens to them confirms that story. But we all have experiences that could support a very different life story. In reviewing his entire life, a man who does not feel confident in social situations can almost certainly recall instances where he handled social situations with skill and aplomb. From these he could construct a different life story.

Have you ever noticed the inner voice that comments on your

actions: "Boy, was that a dumb thing to do," or "You handled that pretty well"? This inner voice is called *self-talk*, and it can either support our efforts or tear us down. In chapter 13 I discuss how we can learn to pay attention to our self-talk and edit it to support our efforts to change.

We think of ourselves as having a single personality. But psychologists tell us that our personalities consist of many subpersonalities. What if the basis for a conflict with your partner is a result of one aspect of your personality tangling with an aspect of your partner's personality, while other aspects of your personalities aren't even disagreeing? Sound wild? Check out chapter 14 to learn how subpersonalities can become entangled.

As I discuss in chapter 15, people and relationships are made up of many different parts and experiences, and this can create conflict or can be a way to build strength. The challenge is to learn to draw on the strengths of each unique person and their qualities to meet life's inevitable tests.

The conclusion offers a quick summary of the guidelines presented in this book.

My suggestion to couples is that both of you first read the entire book and then talk over how much of it you think applies to the two of you. The critical element is whether you both understand that you participate in creating your own emotional reality and believe that it is possible to find new ways to interpret events that accommodate both of you. Read the skills section with care, because these skills will enable you to discover new meanings in your experiences. I recommend that you work on these skills first, then review the tools and approaches in part 3 and select whichever approaches seem most effective for you.

Trying all the approaches discussed in this book may take weeks, months, or even longer. Some of us who started down this path are still on it years later. But it has been worth it. To understand and gain control over the meanings you attach to life is a constantly fulfilling process. It begins with understanding and accepting responsibility for creating your own reality, as discussed in the next two chapters.

Summary

The goal of this book is to help reduce conflicts between couples, especially conflicts based on different perceptions of reality. These conflicts are rooted in the simple fact that we each have our own way of perceiving reality. Disagreements, maybe even fights, are inevitable. Conflict arises when we blame these differences on defects in other people's personalities, moral sense, or compassion. The solution is to explore ways to share our lives even though we experience separate realities. Using the skills and approaches in this book, you can learn to use the differences in your individual perceptions to develop a deeper, more harmonious relationship.

CHAPTER TWO

Making Sense

The minute we're born — perhaps even sooner — we begin trying to make sense of things. Most of the time it seems like what we need to learn is "out there," external to our skin. What makes sense seems predefined; it is our job to discover it. We don't realize that what is "in here" — inside ourselves — plays a major role in the way we make sense of things.

Humans are "sense-making" creatures. This doesn't mean that our explanations for events and feelings actually make sense. A perfect example is the five-year-old who holds himself responsible for his parents' divorce. We can understand how a child can come up with this explanation, but to other people, it doesn't make sense. A child usually plays little or no role in the issues that divide a couple. The child didn't cause the breakup and can't keep the parents together, but he may still feel responsible.

Children are not alone in coming up with explanations based on incomplete or inaccurate information. We've all had the experience of getting upset, only to discover that our upset was based upon an incomplete understanding or a false interpretation of circumstances. Usually we just experience a momentary embarrassment — oops! — and move on. But we often fail to realize that *all* our interpretations of events are the product of what we think we know.

I recently saw the story of William Crawford, a janitor at the US Air Force Academy. Crawford pushed his broom and cleaned his toilets day after day. He was quiet and unassuming, so little attention was paid to him. Then one day a cadet doing some research on World War II found evidence that Crawford might have been awarded the Medal of Honor. This is the army's highest honor. All uniformed personnel, including generals, are expected to salute any winner of the medal. The recipient's children automatically receive free admission to any of the military academies. It's a big deal.

The cadet was able to confirm that William Crawford had indeed been awarded the Medal of Honor. Fighting in Italy, Crawford had single-handedly wiped out three German machine-gun nests, allowing his platoon to capture a key mountain position. But he had been captured and was thought to have been killed. As a result he had never been officially handed his medal. Once his background was discovered, Air Force Academy staff arranged to have President Ronald Reagan present him with his medal. However, he continued to work as a janitor at the academy for some years. He's now the only person not from the Air Force who is buried on Air Force Academy property.

Imagine interacting with a janitor, perhaps even ordering him around, and then being told he was a Medal of Honor recipient. How embarrassing! Once people learned about his Medal of Honor, their understanding of who they were dealing with was altered forever, and so were their feelings toward him.

Art often illuminates life. Akira Kurosawa's classic film *Rashomon* tells the story of a dramatic murder. The story is reenacted four times from the perspectives of four different characters. It's not just the narration of the events that changes: as each character tells the story, its meaning changes too. Viewers develop very strong emotions based on their first understanding of the situation. Their sense-making behavior is fully engaged, providing an interpretation of what is going on. When they have access to more information and the situation differently, their feelings change. They may even be embarrassed by their initial feelings.

This same kind of dramatic shift occurs sometimes when couples share their painful experiences with one another. Understanding the pain of abuse, the crushing burden of an overly controlling parent, or the shame associated with perpetual poverty can help a person understand why their partner views reality the way they do.

In other words, feelings are not the result of external circumstances alone. We give events a meaning based on our expectations, beliefs, thoughts, and past history. If we acquire more information, or a new perspective, our feelings about the events change, even though the events do not.

Other people play a crucial role in shaping the way we ascribe meaning to events. As small children, we depend almost entirely on family members to help us decide what things mean. As we grow older, schools play a crucial role. Throughout our lives, friends and relatives continue to shape our interpretation of events, as does the culture in which we live. We all play a role in telling each other what things mean.

Sociologists and psychologists describe the groups of people around us who influence our thinking as our "interpretive communities." Families, in particular, create a culture or story. Family rules determine who gets to say what they think and feel (usually parents) and who should stay quiet (children). In some families, everyone is taught to avoid confrontation. Other families have a style of dealing with conflict very directly and openly, including children. Families have unwritten rules about what role each parent should play in child-rearing.

In schools we are taught that we are good or poor students. We learn subtle differences in status, so that we know who the cool kids are. We are also taught how to feel about other people and other countries. In some cultures, schools and institutions emphasize respect for authority. Others stress the virtues of equality.

Marshall McLuhan, one of the mid-twentieth century's important thinkers, once claimed that culture is like a glass dome. As long as you are inside it, you don't know that you are enclosed. If everyone around us has the same beliefs, then we don't notice that our feelings may not be universal — that they may be rooted in our family, community, or culture.

One way to see that feelings are based on beliefs that are not universal is to watch attitudes change socially. Probably no change in recent American culture is more dramatic than the position of women. Since the 1970s there have been radical changes in beliefs about the role of women in families and society. Women have often felt conflicted about their own aspirations and social expectations: they may feel they should have a career, but they also feel they should have children and spend time with them. A woman who changes her ideas about her family role needs her partner to change also.

As social and cultural beliefs change, so do our emotions.

Self-Fulfilling Prophecies

One of the challenges in exploring how our ingrained beliefs influence our perceptions and emotions is that the process is nearly instantaneous. It happens so fast that we're not aware we're reaching a feeling based on our judgment, which is based on our beliefs. More than that, once we've accepted a belief, it not only tells us what to feel; it also drives our behavior. We act on that belief, and our beliefs often become *self-fulfilling prophecies*.

A self-fulfilling prophecy is a thought that makes us act in a way that brings about the expected outcome. In other words, because we expect something to happen, we act in ways that bring about what we expect, and that outcome in turn seems to prove that our expectation was correct.

Joanie and David have been married for nearly ten years, and Joanie has come to expect David to be distant and aloof, not show interest, not talk, not kiss, not touch, not notice her. She feels rejected. Even though she wants emotional contact, when they get home from work she acts as though he has already rejected her. Because she expects him to be distant, she begins to feel hurt the minute he walks in the door, and she begins poking at him with caustic digs. He feels attacked, so he shuts down, fulfilling her expectation. Joanie has little awareness of the role she plays in making him emotionally distant. He might be distant anyway, but we may never find out, because she's so busy giving him good reasons to act that way. Feeling rejected, she acts in ways that ensure her rejection.

Imagine how things might be different if she said: "I'd like to feel close to you. I'd like to give you a big hug and talk for a few minutes." An approach like this might get Joanie the response from David that she wants.

In a self-fulfilling prophecy, our deep and strongly held beliefs influence our actions toward others. Those actions in turn trigger beliefs in other people that motivate their actions toward us. These actions prove to us that we were right in the first place.

Here's a simple example:

Several people take a course that might help them get a promotion. To get credit, they need to get a grade of B. They all took a test partway through the course, and each received a C.

Bill is deeply discouraged by his C. He tells himself, "I'm no good at taking tests. I can't even do well in this rinky-dink course." Bill is so discouraged that he gives up trying. The result is that he gets a D in the course. Because he thinks he's no good academically, he proves it.

Judith is disappointed in her C. She tells herself, "I'm usually pretty good at this stuff, and this is just a midterm test. I bet if I work really hard I can bring this grade up to a B." So she works hard and gets a B, just barely missing out on an A. She knows she can do well if she works hard, and proves it.

Regina is angry with her C. She believes the teacher doesn't like her. This belief could direct her behavior in at least two ways. She could decide, "I'm going to show her," work hard, and get a good grade. Or she could conclude that because of the teacher's dislike her efforts are hopeless, give up, and get a poor grade. Regina decides it is hopeless to try to do well in a course when the teacher doesn't like her. She gives up trying and does poorly in the rest of the course.

All three people had the same external experience: getting a C on the test. But they each had a different emotional reaction to the event, and they took different actions based on their feelings. Bill, for example, has proved to himself that he can't be expected to do well in a classroom setting. Judith has proved that she is a good student as long as she puts out the effort. Regina does nothing to give the teacher a reason to like her, and increasingly brings about the poor outcome she expects.

Not only does our interpretation of events cause us to act in certain ways, but our actions in turn cue other people to act the way we expect them to act. The result proves to us that we were right all along.

In ancient Greek mythology, Pygmalion was a sculptor who fell in love with one of his sculptures, which then came to life. Psychologists use the term *Pygmalion effect* to describe how our expectations cause others to act in ways that fulfill our expectations, even when we are unaware of how we are influencing them. For example, a leader's high expectations may lead to an improvement in her followers' performance. (The opposite of the Pygmalion effect is the *golem effect*, in which low expectations lead to declining performance.)

In a dramatic illustration of the Pygmalion effect, all the students in one class in school were given IQ tests. During the summer vacation, the researchers met with the teachers and told them that certain students were expected to be "intellectual bloomers" the coming year and gave the teachers the names of those students. Actually, those students had been selected at random. There was no reason to expect them to perform better than any other student. At the end of the study, students were given the IQ test once again. The students who had been identified as "bloomers" did much better than the rest of the students, even though the teachers were unaware of treating the bloomers differently. The teachers' expectations that these students would perform better somehow got transmitted to the students and led to better performance. This research was conducted in the 1960s and would no longer be considered ethical. But it did create a much greater understanding of the extent to which teacher expectations affect student performance.

Encouraging the Behavior We Want from Others

Our expectations cue other people's behavior, even when we are not aware of it. It pays to be aware of our expectations and even consider changing them in order to encourage the behavior we want from others.

Inez tells the story of taking charge of her actions in order to bring about the behavior she wanted:

For many years I felt hurt that my mother never told me "I love you." I knew that this had not been done in her family and she had never been comfortable saying these words to us children. I'd picked up the family behavior and had trouble telling people I cared about that I loved them. As a trainer of others in communication skills, I thought I ought to "walk the walk." After working on myself, I realized that I was able to say "I love you" to all the important people in my life, except my mother. Many experiences and expectations got in my way.

I decided to live up to what I was teaching in my classes and say "I love you" to my mother. I faced the fact that by not saying "I love you," I was withholding what she had not given me. I wanted to act right regardless of her response. She was at least eighty years old at the time. The next time I saw her and blew a kiss goodbye to her ear, I said, "I love you." She made no response. From that point on whenever I said goodbye to her I said, "I love you." The second time, I think I heard a grunt; she was obviously very uncomfortable. Within a few months, and before I lost her to senility, she learned to say, "I love you too." I felt better about myself, and because I felt better about myself I also felt better about her.

Inez was stuck in her hurt and anger. Things began to happen when she decided to take charge of her behavior in order to get the change she wanted. To do that, she had to let go of the expectation that her mother would say "I love you." We all need to re-examine the meanings we give to events and take responsibility if our behaviors do not result in the behavior we want from others.

Inez had to act alone, without asking or expecting her mother to change. Even so, her change brought results. Think how much more powerful it can be when two people — maybe you and your partner — work together to understand how their unconscious interpretations influence their relationship. That's where we are going next.

Summary

Feelings are not the result of external circumstances alone. We give events a meaning based on our expectations, beliefs, thoughts, and past history. These meanings, in turn, dictate our feelings. If we are given more information or a new perspective, our feelings may change, even though the external events remain the same. We all play a role in telling each other what things mean. Once we've accepted a belief, that meaning not only tells us what to feel; it also drives our behavior. We act on that belief, and our beliefs often become *self-fulfilling prophecies*. Not only does our interpretation of events cause us to act in certain ways, but the ways we act also cue other people to act in the way we expect. We can learn to adapt our own behavior to encourage the behavior we want from others.

CHAPTER THREE

Creating Reality

We each create our own emotional reality. We do this by attributing meaning, significance, and value to the events in our lives. Then we engage in actions that encourage other people to confirm our expectations. Our emotional realities allow us, to some degree, to predict events and exercise control over our life experiences.

Problems arise when we make the mistake of assuming that the reality we experience is objective, determined only by events "out there." When we have been deeply hurt by another person, the intensity of our pain seems like tangible proof that that person deliberately meant to injure us. It isn't easy to see that our experience of that event is determined by our inner emotional reality as much as, or more than, by the other person's behavior.

The idea that we create our own emotional reality is counterintuitive. Most of the time we experience our emotions as being caused by external events. This idea is also reinforced by our culture. For example, songs with words like "You make me feel like dancing" reinforce the belief that our feelings are entirely determined by other people and outside events.

We end up seeing ourselves as the passive recipients of outside information. But when those interpretations of reality make our relationships painful, it's time to slow down and consider whether our interpretations really make sense.

What's "Out There"

Recent neuroscience research supports the view that we generate our reality rather than simply react to external events (see sidebar).

WHAT DOES NEUROSCIENCE SAY ABOUT HOW WE CREATE REALITY?

Because our emotions mostly seem to arise without any apparent conscious thought, we're convinced that external events cause our feelings. For many years, scientific research operated on the same assumption. But recent neuroscience research tells us otherwise. Anil Seth, professor of cognitive and computational neuroscience at the University of Sussex in the United Kingdom, has summarized the latest neuroscience research as follows: instead of perception depending on signals coming into the brain from the outside world, it depends as much, if not more, on perceptual predictions flowing in the opposite direction. We don't just passively perceive the world, we actively create it. The world of experience comes as much, if not more, from the inside out as from the outside in.

According to Dr. Seth, as the brain receives information, it "predicts" what that information means on the basis of thousands, perhaps millions, of prior experiences.

Most events in our everyday experience recur so frequently that these predictions have great accuracy. But,
even so, the brain is constantly refining these predictions.
When exposed to new experiences and events, the brain
generates multiple predictions, based on experience, and
then selects and refines these predictions in response to
new information.

In his lectures to students in Britain, Dr. Seth illus-
trates how the brain generates predictions by playing a
recording in which everything the speaker says is garbled
and unintelligible. He plays it again. It still cannot be de-
ciphered. Then he plays a recording in which the same
speaker clearly says, "I think Brexit is a really terrible
idea." Finally he replays the original recording. This time
listeners can clearly make out the words "I think Brexit is
a really terrible idea."

The recording didn't change. But now that the brain
has more information, it fills in the words. What we are
hearing is based both on what is actually said and the
brain's prediction, based on the information obtained
from the second recording.

In other words, your brain plays a much more active
role in shaping your experiences than you may realize.
According to Lisa Feldman Barrett, a professor of psychology at Northeastern University:

> Your control network...constantly shapes the
> course of your predictions and prediction error
> to help select among multiple actions, whether
> you experience yourself as in control or not.
> This network can only work with the concepts

that you've got. So the question of responsibility becomes, Are you responsible for your concepts? Not all of them, certainly. When you're a baby, you can't choose the concepts that other people put into your head. But as an adult, you absolutely do have choices about what you expose yourself to and therefore what you learn, which creates the concepts that ultimately drive your actions, whether they feel willful or not. So "responsibility" means making deliberate choices to change your concepts.

Since much of what we experience is generated inside the brain, it is inevitable that my reality and yours will be dissimilar, sometimes significantly. But we do have the opportunity to influence the predictions the brain makes until we can find a meaning that works for both of us.

Even though each of us has a unique emotional reality, it doesn't mean that there is not a shared reality out there. When we see a car racing toward us as we cross a street, the perception triggers a response of fear or caution, prompting us to take action to avoid getting hit. We did not create the event — the reckless driver or the speeding car — but we do create a unique emotional reaction to it. One individual may be over the experience as soon as the body's physiology — a rush of adrenaline, rapid breathing, etc. — quiets down. For another person, this may be a traumatic experience that disturbs them for days.

When two people in a close relationship have different reactions to events, it can be disturbing. For some people, it is so scary that it threatens the relationship. Those differences in emotional reality are inevitable. The message of this book is that you don't have to have the same reactions to be close. In fact, those differences may be part of a joint learning experience.

Summary

Most of the time we experience our emotions as caused by external events. But when those interpretations of reality start making our relationships painful, it's time to slow down and consider whether our interpretations really make sense. Recent neuroscience research supports the view that we generate our own reality rather than simply react to external events. Since much of what we experience is generated inside our own brain, it is inevitable that my reality and yours will differ. But we can influence the predictions the brain makes until we can find a meaning that works for us.

CHAPTER FOUR

Using Differences as Teachers

When we get close to another person, we quickly discover that their emotional reality is not exactly like ours. At this point, a struggle often begins over who is "right." Arguments over whose emotional reality is right are often particularly painful and long lasting.

Here's an example of a conflict over emotional realities:

Ron was raised in a family where great emphasis was placed on family loyalty. His mother and father had married against their parents' wishes and often felt beleaguered and isolated from others in the community. Their unifying myth, or family story, was that everyone disapproved of them, and as their family grew, all its members developed the belief that they had to defend each other against every outsider. In practice, Ron's family operated with a shared belief that "if you love me, you will not call attention to any of my shortcomings. In return, and as an expression of my love for you, I will not call attention to any of your shortcomings."

Ron's wife, Priscilla, was raised in a very close family, where feelings were expressed openly, if sometimes loudly. The role of family members was seen as "improving" each other, helping them to be more successful in life, rather than blindly defending and protecting each other. The shared family belief was, "If you love me, you will give me constructive feedback about my mistakes, and I will try to improve myself. I will show my love for you by giving you constructive feedback whenever I think you can profit from it." This behavior also extended to others: as friends came to be thought of as part of the family, they too would receive criticism.

During their courtship, Ron was attracted to Priscilla because she was warm and expressive, while she liked him because he seemed very self-reliant and independent. This was particularly important to her because she found it hard to break away from her family, often feeling pulled and torn by their demands.

But now, after a few years of marriage, Ron and Priscilla both feel hurt and rejected. When Priscilla engages in what she believes to be loving behavior — pointing out how Ron might be more successful at work, or why the kids do not pay more attention to him — he responds as if he has been attacked.

Ron experiences her attempts at constructive criticism as attempts to undermine and hurt him. In particular, if she criticizes him in front of close friends, he feels embarrassed and betrayed. Priscilla feels hurt and rejected because anytime she tries to be loving and supportive, by pointing out ways that Ron could improve, he reacts as if she were cruel and mean. She also is beginning to worry that Ron does not really love her, because he fails to support her by showing her how she could improve.

Because Ron and Priscilla accept beliefs instilled in them by their families, their efforts to express love are at cross-purposes. Both of them act in ways they believe are loving, but each sees the other as unloving.

This conflict rests on two fundamentally different understandings of what it means to tell a partner about shortcomings.

Ron believes that Priscilla's habit of correcting his shortcomings is hurtful criticism, undermining him and making him feel unloved. He also believes that criticism fundamentally threatens the security of the relationship. Priscilla, on the other hand, believes that correcting Ron's shortcomings is a sign of how much she loves him. When Ron won't correct her own shortcomings, she interprets his behavior as a sign that he doesn't care about her.

Ron and Priscilla learned these beliefs in their families of origin. Questioning these beliefs is seen as criticizing or even rejecting each other's families.

Guidelines for Learning from Differences

This is not a disagreement that is going to end quickly. It won't be resolved by trying to prove who is right. How could Ron and Priscilla deal with their differences without the estrangement or sense of distance caused by this fight? How can you build a shared life when there are such differences?

The solution lies in employing a new style of communication that respects the partners' separate emotional realities, allowing each to maintain the integrity of their individual truths and to express their own reality without fear. It follows eleven guidelines that are the basis for the rest of this book and that will help you see your differences as a teacher rather than as a source of conflict.

1. Agree that each person has a right to his or her way of seeing and experiencing things (his or her emotional reality) while affirming and trusting your own.

Each of you respects the other's emotional reality, rather than defending your own point of view as the only truth. As long as you are fighting over who is right, or labeling each other as irrational, misguided, or emotionally disturbed, nothing can come from the conflict except more conflict. Your feelings are valid and a part of your own truth, but those feelings can change quickly if you gain a new understanding of the events that led to those feelings.

The starting point is to accept it as a fact that two people can experience the same event in very different ways. Accept it as a fact that the other person's feelings make perfect sense within their emotional reality — within their life experiences — and that this is okay.

While many of us accept these principles in our heads, most of us still have difficulty accepting them in our hearts.

2. Communicate your own reality without finding fault with other people's.

Our interpretations may be 100 percent right for us even while being largely unworkable for others. We choose how we see reality, but we need not insist that others see it the same way. We can give up the belief that having other people agree with us is a test of love and give up the fear that when others see things differently, it's a sign that they don't love us.

Chapter 5 provides guidelines for communicating in new ways that leave room for each other's differences. It introduces the concept of *response-ability* — the ability to respond — that enables us to recognize and avoid communication styles rooted in blame or judgment. Response-ability requires learning that while we have feelings and beliefs, we are not wholly identified with them. We concentrate instead on communicating feelings and the meanings that create them. Even when the other person's communication is seen as provocative, we can make choices about how we respond.

3. Listen — with both your head and your heart — even though you may continue to disagree.

When we are engaged in conflict with someone who has a very different emotional reality, there is a tendency to feel threatened or fearful. We begin to see the other person as an alien and as an abstraction; this view is often expressed in phrases such as "You're always doing that" or "That's just like a man to do that!" This may escalate into seeing the other person as an aggressor, out to get us, filled with evil motives. When we begin to see the other person as an adversary or even as an enemy, we engage in behavior that makes this belief a self-fulfilling prophecy. As our vision narrows and we see only undesirable traits in the other person, our behavior encourages those undesirable traits in them. Often we believe our pain is proof that the other person is the cruel adversary we have created in our own mind's eye. In fact, this creature is of our own creation.

There is another possible path: practicing *empathy*. Empathy is the ability to experience — at least to some degree — what the other person is experiencing. This can help you understand how it would feel to be in the other person's reality. It doesn't mean that you take the other person's position; you are simply allowing yourself to experience what it would be like to do so. Empathy allows us to enter into the emotional reality of our loved ones, so that even when there are differences there is still shared experience.

Chapter 7 concludes with a summary of basic listening skills, with an emphasis on *active listening*. This is a skill that allows you to accept others' emotional realities while maintaining the integrity of your own perceptions. If these skills take us to strange places, at least we are traveling with someone who loves us and knows the way.

4. Learn to identify behaviors that cause fights to escalate, and set mutually acceptable rules to limit these behaviors.

Fights, particularly between couples, can start over the silliest of things. Sadly, these squabbles can escalate to the point where both people feel hurt, angry, and rejected.

Fights don't blow out of control all by themselves. They escalate because of the behaviors in which both parties engage. There is even a predictable pattern to escalation. Each person is justifying their own behavior as just getting even for what the other person said or did. That really means that neither person is taking responsibility for their own behavior.

In chapter 8 we identify the predictable steps in escalation and look at the behaviors that make fights go from bad to worse. We also discuss some simple ground rules that can prevent fights from escalating.

5. Use a problem-solving process that says "We have a problem," not "You are the problem."

Many people try to solve problems starting with the belief that their partner is the barrier to solving the problem. The chances of finding a mutually acceptable solution will be very limited if each sees the other as an opponent. By changing the basis of the discussion to "*We* have a problem," a couple can greatly expand the range of alternative solutions they can consider.

Chapter 9 presents the steps in a structured problem-solving process. A process like this helps you focus on "We." It also demonstrates the essentials of arriving at an outcome that is acceptable to both partners.

6. Look for the positive good that your partner supports, even when your partner opposes what you think is important.

Most of the really tough decisions in life are not choices between good and bad but between two good things that compete or are in tension with each other. Accepting a promotion in another city, for example, may help you financially and further your career, but these benefits come at the price of close relationships you and your children have built in the community where you live now. Career advancement is good, but so are the relationships you've built.

That's what makes many decisions difficult: you have to decide which good thing is more important than other good things. The real decision is which choice is most important in a particular situation. Usually we agree on the things that are good, but we disagree about the relative weight or importance to give them.

These choices are called *values choices*, because they involve trade-offs between different things that we value. They often arise over decisions about spending money. What value should be given to things we can enjoy now, and what value to saving up for the future? Is it worthwhile to spend money on a fancy car, or should we spend only enough money for a car that is serviceable?

Many of the conflicts between couples involve exactly this kind of decision-making. Our preferred choices reflect the values that we think are most important in a given situation. Each decision requires balancing two or more goods.

When we argue about what action to take, we frequently see our partner as someone who opposes what we believe to be right; conversely, the partner may feel that we are discounting the value and importance of a different choice. The key principle for dealing with values differences is to recognize that your partner is not opposing you but simply giving different relative weights to values you both support.

7. Seek out new ways of perceiving reality you can both agree on.

When we are faced with external facts, we interpret the facts, and we do so in a context that we create ourselves. We "frame" the situation through our deeply held beliefs and assumptions.

Old ways of framing our experiences may place us under unnecessary constraints. They can prevent us from exploring and using our own abilities to our best advantage. They may even be responsible for the impasse between partners with different emotional realities.

If you and your partner have a continuing struggle, you may be able to break the impasse by reframing the situation, finding alternative ways of understanding it that can accommodate both partners' emotional realities.

8. Reframe your life story as needed to create options and free up capabilities.

One way to change your life is to revise the story you tell yourself about it. By looking for past events that contradict the way you think about your life now, you may be able to reclaim parts of yourself and craft a new story that accommodates both your emotional reality and your partner's. You may find that you can act in ways that you never imagined possible.

9. Examine your self-talk to be sure it is serving you well, and reprogram it when you need to.

We all have an inner voice that comments on what we are doing, favorably or otherwise. Psychologists refer to this inner dialogue as *self-talk*. We learn most of our self-talk as children, from parents and other adults. Some self-talk serves us well, and some of it imposes constraints on our behavior that don't serve us as adults.

A great deal of this self-talk is negative. Changing your negative self-talk is a powerful way of changing your beliefs about yourself, including your attitudes to and behaviors around conflict.

10. Get to know the different parts of your personality and get them talking to each other.

Most of us think of ourselves as a single, unitary personality. Yet we often experience divisions that make us feel torn, as if there are separate and distinct personalities warring within us. We even describe it that way: "One part of me says I should go ahead and do it, but another part of me cautions me against it."

Resolving disputes over differing emotional realities involves learning to recognize these different parts of ourselves and noticing which one is in charge at any given time. In chapter 14 we explore the dynamics of personality that may be the basis for why we have the particular emotional reality we have, and why we feel the need to defend it the way we do.

11. Accept that differences can make your relationships richer.

Our differences with another person become teachers when we see ourselves, individually and as a couple, as being on a search for truth. Along the way you may discover truths, but no human being yet knows "the Truth." Sharing the search, even when you face differences, can strengthen your relationship.

One of the great rewards of this joint search is that the other person may possess a truth that can improve the quality of your life as you incorporate it into your own truth.

Look for principles or new ways of perceiving reality that are large enough to contain both people's versions of the truth. Finally, end the struggle when you are able to agree on a new, shared version of the truth — "our" truth. In this way you honor both your own truth and the truth of your partner. You've used your differences as a teacher, leading you to a deeper mutual understanding and richer love.

The following chapters address these guidelines. Some chapters describe skills that require practice to master. This practice offers another opportunity to use differences as a teacher.

Summary

Arguments over whose emotional reality is right are often particularly painful and long-lasting. They can be resolved by employing a new style of communication that respects both partners' different emotional realities, allowing each person to maintain the integrity of their individual truths and express their reality without fear.

PART TWO

SKILLS

CHAPTER FIVE

Response-ability

Agree that each person has a right to his or her
way of seeing and experiencing things
(his or her emotional reality) while affirming
and trusting your own.

I f you want to free yourself from conflict with a partner arising
from different realities, the first step is to explore the meanings
and interpretations you bring to the relationship. If those meanings and interpretations are no longer serving you well, search for
new truths that serve you better.

As we discussed in chapter 2, our feelings are not caused by
external events alone. When someone says something to us and
we then experience a feeling, it seems as if it is the comment that
causes our feeling. But feelings arise only when we interpret or
give meaning to an event, such as another person's comment. This
interpretation typically happens so fast that we aren't aware of it.
It is an unconscious process. There's survival value in this. When
a saber-toothed tiger leaped out of the bushes, our ancestors were

not well served by long deliberations about what its arrival meant.

Every now and then something happens — maybe it is a story we've just seen on the news — and we don't know what it is going to mean for us. As a result, we don't know what we feel. The event alone is not enough, without the meaning, to tell us what to feel.

I remember this happening when we had teenage children, back before there were cell phones. When they went out with friends or on a date, they might be an hour late getting home, and we had no idea what might have happened to them. We could be terrified one moment, then angry. We wouldn't really know how we felt until they came home and provided an explanation.

Our unconscious interpretation of events happens so quickly that we are often unaware of it. But this process can be slowed down for conscious examination. We can take charge of it and learn new ways of interpreting events that open up new choices about feelings and actions.

Reaction is immediate and unthinking. Response is a choice. Those of us who have not yet examined the meanings we bring to our relationships can only react. We are not free to respond. In a very real way, we are hostages to our own beliefs. We can, however, teach ourselves not to automatically react out of our old interpretations. We gain "response-ability" by making our interpretations more conscious.

One person described learning response-ability as follows: "If something happened that I didn't know how to handle, I would freeze, as if facing a physical threat. I have learned to recognize my body's response to a threat and to override my freeze response by knowing that if I shift my body slightly or speak up and move around, I can break the freeze. And then my brain is able to take over again."

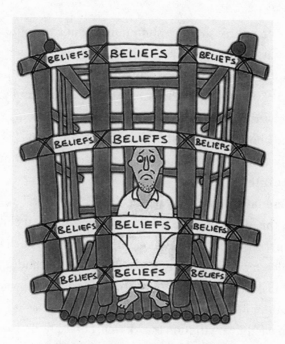

When we learn response-ability,
we are no longer the prisoner of our beliefs.

Learning response-ability can be done working alone, or with a counselor; but when both people in a relationship commit themselves to this process, it is easier and faster. By sharing the insights as well as the frustrations of this effort, you will also feel closer to each other.

Family Myths

In our early years we develop our perceptions of reality through our families. Every family shares some basic assumptions about the world. In fact, it is the willingness to accept these assumptions that helps the individual belong to or have "membership" in the family. Often these shared assumptions are not verbalized, or the family may not have openly examined them. Because they are typically not conscious, they are sometimes referred to by people in the field of psychology as the "family trance" or as "family myths." These myths may encompass rules about closeness or separateness and about what is just or fair, or right or wrong. They may prescribe rules for marital power sharing and for communicating love or worth.

These myths often define our sense of the ideal partner or spouse, the ideal marriage, the ideal family, the ideal child. Each of us carries these expectations from the family in which we grew up. We learn our future family roles while we are children — unless we make the family myth conscious and choose whether or not to adopt it.

Some family myths don't work well. For example, many families in which one or both parents abuse alcohol or are mentally ill create myths that permit the family to deny this reality. This can often lead to the children abusing alcohol or being attracted to a partner who does so or is mentally ill.

Each partner brings their family myths into a relationship. Even if we believe we have achieved some degree of separation from our families, these beliefs may continue to shape our relationships because we carry them forward without reexamination.

Here's an example.

Judy's family proudly identifies as working class. This involves much more than the historical fact that they have worked in the steel mills for three generations. The family actively discourages behavior that is inconsistent with this working-class identity. Only certain cars are considered acceptable. No one would be caught dead with a glass of wine when there's beer available. There's pressure for family members not to get "above themselves" by getting too much education, buying fancy homes, or "acting like something they're not." For Judy's family, success means being respected and liked by other working-class people.

Judy stretched the limits of the family myth when she went to the state university and earned a bachelor's degree. While there, she met and fell in love with Dave, whose father is a senior marketing manager for a Fortune 500 corporation. Dave's father is the second generation of an immigrant family and has made it to his present position by dint of hard work. He doesn't have a college degree: in fact, he had to drop out of college to support his parents when the company his father worked for went out of business. The family is proud of Dave, who is the first person in their family to get a college degree.

At Dave and Judy's wedding, there was obvious tension between the families. Many of Dave's parents' suggestions for the wedding were interpreted by Judy's family as signs that Dave's family didn't think them good enough. To avoid this tension, Dave and Judy accepted jobs in a city some distance from both families. They like to think they have escaped from their families, but both feel isolated without the strong family support they once enjoyed.

With both Judy and Dave working, they can afford two new cars and even a new house. But each time they make a decision to make such a purchase, painful conflict erupts between them. What Dave sees as a reward for getting ahead, Judy sees as pretension. She even experiences a vague sense of disloyalty to her family. When Judy and Dave try to talk about these issues, their discussions often turn into bitter attacks of each other's families, with many accusations and counteraccusations about caring more about approval from their families than about the other person.

Family myths create a sense of belonging. Adherence to the myths is a form of bonding. When the myths are challenged — when we think, feel, or act differently than the myth dictates — we may feel that we are traitors or that we are rejecting our families, and we may in turn feel isolated from or rejected by our families. Even when no family members are around to enforce the family beliefs, our inner voices effectively police our efforts to break away.

Judy's family defines itself by its commitment to its working-class origins. Now that Dave and Judy are family, she sees his upwardly mobile behavior as an attack on her family and feels guilty if she participates in it.

For Dave, Judy's insistence on maintaining working-class ways is incomprehensible. Dave's immigrant family has struggled for three generations to escape poverty and everything associated with it. Dave feels that his wife should support him in acquiring the visible proof that his family has finally made it. When she does not provide this support, he interprets her reaction as "wallowing in irrational guilt." Both Dave and Judy feel that the myths that define their families of origin are under attack, but neither is conscious of how much of their identity is tied up in these family myths.

Family myths play a large role in the ways we learn to handle conflict. I was raised in a family in which conflicts just weren't "done." Nobody talked about disagreements, and any child who brought them up was shamed. Conflicts remained underground. This family myth taught the children to avoid conflict and to suppress and distrust their own feelings. Avoidance, even suppression, of conflict was combined with a belief that the wife's role was to be submissive to the husband. An imbalance of power in the relationship was built into the family by culture and reinforced by religion — at least on the surface. In reality, my mother did a great deal of maneuvering and manipulation until my father acknowledged her concerns.

My wife was raised in a family in which the predominant value was to stand up for oneself. This required open and often loud statement of opinions and judgments. Feuds were common: it almost required a scorecard to keep track of who was talking to whom. And conflicts didn't seem to get resolved; family members just pulled away from each other.

I brought my family's rules into our marriage, and my wife brought hers. After some bitter and hurtful fights — and marriage counseling — we began to set our own rules for handling conflicts. We set limits on the behaviors we engaged in during fights. For example, realizing that timing can be very important, we agreed on how to decide when we would discuss issues. She always wanted to talk about everything right away. I usually avoided discussing the issue as long as possible. Eventually I agreed that we would always talk about the issue, but at a mutually acceptable time within twenty-four hours. We agreed not to expand the fight from whatever was the original issue, to just stick with one subject and put other issues aside until another time. We agreed not to use other people's comments as ammunition, and to discuss only our own thoughts and feelings rather than bringing in what other people might think or say. Those were our issues; yours may be entirely different.

The only escape from disagreement over family rules is to agree on your own rules. Just accept that each partner brings a different set of rules to the relationship. As long as these two sets of rules remain unexpressed, they will conflict.

Identify the behaviors that bother you. Then discuss a way of behaving that is acceptable to you both. Each person should think about these things independently; then you can talk about them together and try out your new rules for a while. From time to time you may need to assess how well the rules are working.

Because rules for handling conflict may be part of family

myths about what kind of people we are, changing the rules may also require reexamining those myths and changing at least part of how we've defined ourselves in the past.

In the end, myths are just that — myths. They help us organize our lives and assign meaning to our experiences, but sometimes they cease to be useful. When that happens, we turn from the old myths and seek new beliefs that can help us make sense of our lives.

Other Meanings

In addition to family myths, there are other sets of assumptions and beliefs that shape the meanings we bring to relationships.

Gender Roles

The meaning of gender is under intense debate in our society today. Often the argument has to do with whether gender differences are rooted in physiology, or whether they are learned differences, rooted in social conditioning — or perhaps both.

With respect to behavior in intimate relationships, studies do show that women are more likely to attempt to achieve intimacy by sharing feelings. By contrast, men often feel threatened by feelings, and distance themselves from strong feelings. This begins the dance of the pursuer and the distancer (see chapter 7). Sometimes in a relationship it is the man who is the pursuer and the woman who is the distancer. It depends on personality as well as a sense of being male or female.

Culture

National and ethnic cultures shape our sense of reality in ways we often don't notice. Many beliefs we have about the roles of spouses, children, and families are defined by the culture in which we grew up. When spouses or loved ones come from different cultures, serious conflicts often arise.

For example, in traditional Asian Pacific cultures, the wife is absorbed into her husband's family when she marries; she assumes a status lower than that of her husband and her husband's parents. In traditional Korean culture, the new mother-in-law is in charge of the family. In traditional Japanese families, it is virtuous to be stoic and patient, meeting struggles without complaining. People from these cultures may see American women as forward and aggressive.

Many things we believe to be universally true are, in fact, determined by culture. When we don't recognize our assumptions as coming from our culture but believe they are true for everyone, they may become the source of constant conflict in close relationships.

Personality Type

Personalities form prisms through which people see very different aspects of reality. Our personalities are defined by factors such as our dominant modes of sensory perception (including kinesthetic, visual, and auditory). Some people are introverts, who feel drained of energy after being with people; some are extroverts, who gain energy from being with people. Some people are predominantly intuitive, focusing on emotion, while others are predominantly intellectual, focusing more on thought.

Working Together to Find Shared Meaning

None of us can spend the time to explore and understand all the ways of making meaning we have learned in the past. Many of these processes have great value and make life much easier. In your relationship, start with a limited number of issues where alternative meanings conflict. You may hold many other beliefs that are different from your partner's, but if they aren't the cause of conflict in the relationship, they probably do not need to be addressed.

The critical step is creating a shared commitment to understanding the meanings each of you brings to the relationship. This will happen only if you can create a climate of safety for sharing your deep feelings. Feeling safe means that each of you feels support and encouragement, rather than judgment and blame. You can develop skills for talking to each other that can make it feel safe to share. The next two chapters explore these skills.

Summary

Those of us who have not yet examined the meanings we bring to our relationships can only react; we cannot respond thoughtfully, and thus we are more likely to come into conflict when our meanings differ from another person's. We gain response-ability — the ability to respond rather than react — by making our interpretations more conscious. Ideally, both people in the relationship commit themselves to this self-examination.

We each bring our own family myths, learned from childhood, into our relationships. Because we rarely pause to examine these myths, they continue to shape our relationships, not always in constructive ways. Myths can help us organize our lives and assign meaning to our experiences, but when they cease to be useful, we must turn from the old myths and seek new beliefs.

CHAPTER SIX

Responsible Communication

Communicate your own reality
without finding fault with other people's.

In order for couples to jointly reexamine the meanings that they
give to each other's behavior and find new ways of relating to
each other, they need to share feelings, thoughts, and beliefs at
a very deep level. This requires that both partners feel safe —
meaning that they don't feel judged or criticized for feeling the
way they do.

To create a safe environment, couples need to communicate
responsibly. This means avoiding behaviors that force the other
person into polarized positions. When conflicts get out of control, it is difficult to acknowledge how our own interpretations
may have added to the dispute. Yet it is this kind of behavior that
can move disputes beyond arguments over who is right into intimate sharing about our most important feelings.

Both people must learn to recognize and avoid communication rooted in blame or judgment, concentrating instead on communicating emotions and the meanings that create them. Even

when the other person's communication seems to create conflict, you can make choices about how you respond. If you can imagine that each of you is a country, your job is to describe what's going on in your country rather than interpreting or judging what's going on in the other one.

Suppose you and your partner have had dinner with friends, and you found the evening really boring. To your surprise, you learn that your partner really enjoyed it. If you're a couple who gets into conflict a lot, you could probably find a way to argue over your different experiences of the evening. Soon the argument might escalate into larger issues. Your partner would question your openness to making new friends. You would point out that all they talked about was stupid sporting events, which was pretty adolescent. You would be criticized for always being judgmental, and you would react by criticizing your partner for liking shallow people. And so on.

It is a fact that you felt bored during the evening. It's equally true that your partner enjoyed it. It is not a fact that the interaction was inherently boring, that you correctly interpreted the other couple's interactions, or that your interpretation was the only possible interpretation of the situation. It is a fact that you each have a walking, talking individual emotional reality, and different realities may lead to conflict.

If you feel that you must kill off your partner's reality in order for your reality to survive, you will inevitably get into conflict. Here's the difference between sharing feelings and sharing judgments:

Feelings

Him: I'm was really bored and didn't enjoy the conversation.
Her: I enjoyed myself, and I really liked the people.

Judgments

Him: Those people were really shallow, and it makes my wife look shallow when she says she likes them.

Her: He looks down on everybody. He's incapable of having fun.

Statements expressing feelings are valid and true for the person who expresses them; statements expressing judgment are not necessarily true.

Here's another example of how a conversation is likely to go if you share judgments rather than feelings:

Alice: How could you possibly be so rude? That was just downright mean.

Jorge: I'm being mean? Somebody had to stop that bitch from just running everybody down. Someone had to confront her.

Alice: No polite person ever does that.

Jorge: How come you're sticking up for her when she was just dumping all over both of us? That's really stupid.

Alice: I'm being stupid? Who just embarrassed us in front of all our friends?

Jorge: Why do you think politeness is so all-fired important? I'll take a little honesty any day.

Alice: Are you saying I'm not honest? You bastard.

Here's how a conversation about the same event is likely to go if you share feelings:

Alice: I really felt embarrassed when you said what you did to Irene.

Jorge: I'm sorry you felt embarrassed. I was really getting upset at the way she was putting everybody down. I think I was just being honest about my feelings.

Alice: Well, the way I was raised, that kind of confrontation is considered totally impolite. I'm really embarrassed by anything that's impolite.

Jorge: I can see where your family and my family observed different rules. In my family, what mattered was being honest about feelings.

There's a good chance that coming out of this second conversation, Alice and Jorge may be able to increase their understanding of each other's realities. Maybe they'll discuss why politeness is so important to Alice. Also, they might discuss what it is in Jorge's background that makes him feel he must defend himself and the people around him.

This kind of conversation will help you understand the meanings you ascribe to events, which maybe you've never thought about much before. Once you begin to concentrate on what's going on inside you, and what it means to you, new insights will emerge about why you feel as you do.

Guidelines for Responsible Communication

Here are some basic guidelines for communicating your feelings in a way that reduces defensiveness and reaction.

Take Responsibility for Your Feelings

One of the biggest causes of fights between loved ones is blaming the other person for your feeling: "You made me feel…" As we've discussed, your feelings are not caused by an external event alone, but also by the meaning you give to the event. Those meanings are yours, not the other person's. If we're brutally honest, *you* made you feel whatever you feel.

When you say the other person is responsible for what you feel, that person is likely to feel blamed or accused. They may become defensive and want to protect themselves. We have the beginnings of a full-on battle.

State Feelings, Not Judgments

When we are in conflicts rooted in different perceptions and different emotional realities, it is imperative that we communicate feelings, not judgments. Acknowledging our feelings — feeling hurt, rejected, or angry — is essential to understanding our emotional realities. But expressing judgments — saying that our partner is being unkind, unfair, or cruel — gets in the way. It makes it almost impossible to turn the search for understanding into an exciting joint venture. Instead, both people feel accused, put down, and angry.

Most of us have learned to communicate in what can be called "you" messages, which are often expressions that judge, challenge, or blame the other person, like these:

- "You made me feel..." (blaming the other person for your feelings)
- "You are being..." (judging the other person)
- "Why are you...?" (challenging or questioning the other person)

One way to remind yourself to communicate a feeling, not a judgment, is to start your sentence with "I'm..." or "I feel..." Psychologists and counselors refer to this kind of message as an "I" message. Here is a comparison of "you" messages and "I" messages:

"You" message	"I" message
You made me feel angry when…	I felt angry when…
You are being a jerk.	I'm upset…
Why are you being so defensive?	I felt hurt…

Connect Your Feelings to a Description of the Behavior or Circumstances

It's true that just stating a feeling is not enough. If all Alice says is "I'm embarrassed," Jorge is not going to understand her. Some explanation is needed for why she is embarrassed. But this is a place where judgments can slip in. Efforts to communicate feelings sometimes go awry. For example, Alice might say: "I was really embarrassed when you were so rude." The only word Jorge will hear in that entire sentence is *rude.* That's because Alice has connected her feelings with a big fat judgment. She's mixed an "I" message with a "you" message.

Just putting "I feel" in front of a judgment doesn't make it any less of a judgment. If Alice were to confine her comments to a description of Jorge's behavior, avoiding judgment, she might say: "I really felt embarrassed when you said what you did to Irene." That's an effort to describe Jorge's behavior without judging it.

Tell the Other Person What You Need

Sometimes it's enough for couples to share their feelings about something that has happened; at other times it is helpful for them to tell the each other what they need in order to avoid conflict in the future. For example, when Peter comes home from work, he finds it really upsetting if the house is all messy. Having an orderly environment helps him feel at ease. He'd really like to come home to a tidy house. But he and his wife have three kids, all under seven years old.

Here is Peter's attempt to send an "I" message:

I'm upset when the toys are left on the floor. I really need calm and order when I first get home from work.

He takes responsibility for his feelings by saying "I'm upset," rather than "You are upsetting me."

He tries to communicate a feeling rather than a judgment with "I'm upset" rather than "You're not keeping the kids under control."

He describes a behavior rather than judging it: "when the toys are left on the floor" instead of "when everything is so messy."

And he expresses what he needs: "I really need calm and order when I first get home from work."

To put it another way, you can construct an "I" message as follows:

I'm (or "I feel") _____ [emotion] when _____ [description of behavior or circumstances]. I need _____ [the change you would like to see].

"I" messages do not automatically bring about the result you want. People may still feel upset, hurt, or angry even when you send a good "I" message. Your job is to express your feelings in ways that minimize the risk that the other person will feel the need to react defensively. Their feelings are their own responsibility. If both people send "I" messages, you'll significantly reduce the risk of a fight, or speed the recovery if you are both upset.

The effectiveness of your "I" messages will also be dramatically increased if you combine them with the listening skills discussed in the next chapter.

Summary

Before people are willing to share feelings at a deep level, they need to feel safe, able to express their feelings without worrying about being judged or criticized. To create a safe environment, couples need to take responsibility for how they communicate with each other. One of the biggest causes of fights between loved ones is blaming the other person for your feelings. The first step in making your communication safer is to take ownership of your own feelings and to express feelings rather than judgments. It helps to describe the other person's behavior in neutral terms rather than judging it. Then tell them what you need from the situation.

CHAPTER SEVEN

Listening

Listen — with both your head and your heart — even
though you may continue to disagree.

The single most important skill for finding a shared reality is
listening. No, not the kind where you listen just long enough
to get your reply ready, but genuinely empathetic listening. You
and your partner need to understand each other with your hearts,
not just your heads.

When we are engaged in conflict with people who have very
different emotional realities from our own, there is a tendency
to see the other person not as a loved one but as an adversary.
We feel threatened, and we begin to see the other person as an
abstraction. This is often expressed with phrases such as "You're
always doing that" or "That's just like a man to do that!" This may
lead to reducing the other person to a category or stereotype. We
may begin to see our partner as an aggressor, out to get us, filled
with evil motives.

The other path that is open to us is the path of empathy.
Empathy is the ability to experience — at least in some small

measure — what the other person is experiencing. This path requires a willingness to temporarily suspend our own version of reality and identify with the other person's. Empathy can produce an understanding of how it would feel if you were in the other person's reality. It doesn't mean that you must subscribe to the other person's position; you are simply allowing yourself to experience what it would be like. Empathy allows us to enter into the emotional reality of our loved ones, so that even when there are differences, there can still be sharing.

Pursuers and Distancers

One of the major challenges to developing a shared reality is that it takes a lot of talking about your relationship. Research shows a major difference in the ways women and men approach this task. I do not know whether these differences are rooted in roles we've learned or in biology. Some women may see talking about the relationship as an opportunity to express grievances, while others perhaps hope it is an opportunity to create more connection and understanding. To most men there is no more-dreaded phrase than "We need to talk about our relationship."

Dr. John Gottman has conducted research on couples for more than thirty years. He and his associates have identified a behavior that they call the pursuer/distancer dynamic. Pursuers have a tremendous need to connect and resolve situations, so they keep pushing, urgently trying to get the issue resolved. Distancers try to escape by avoiding talking about the issue. They want physical and emotional distance. Gottman's research shows that women are more likely to be pursuers and men more likely to be distancers.

My wife and I have engaged in this behavior, particularly when we were first married. My wife would push hard to get feelings and problems addressed. Her underlying need was for reassurance and connection. But because of the manner in which she tried to make this connection, often with criticisms, complaints, or challenging questions, I wanted to escape, to avoid any discussion.

My behavior, like that of many men, was to become quiet, turn inward, and avoid problems or conflicts. I would use abstractions, refuse to cooperate, and become rigid and critical of my wife. I actually wanted and needed connection with my wife, but when I felt criticized or questioned, I began to withdraw. Each effort by my wife to establish connection made me withdraw further.

The irony is that both of us were attempting to reduce our anxiety. But as she pushed forward, I pulled back. Each act in which we engaged furthered the distance between us. We were perfect examples of Gottman's pursuer and distancer.

Gottman and his team observed fights between couples and made a number of physiological measurements that could help them estimate the intensity of each person's feelings during the fight. They found that even when the men were stonewalling (completely shutting down), they had feelings that were as strong as or stronger than the women's. The men felt "flooded," overwhelmed by feelings, even if they didn't show them. They shut down to protect themselves from experiencing even more overwhelming feelings and out of a fear that anything they said would make the situation even worse.

To change this dynamic, the pursuer needs to receive affection and soothing, while the distancer needs the space to come forward without feeling criticized. The following behaviors can help:

- Avoid the blame game, in which each partner is looking for things to blame on the other. (Some of the skills described in the previous chapter will help.)

- Remember that people are more willing to share feelings when they feel safe.
- The pursuer can work at self-soothing: that is, calming down without needing to talk it over with the other partner.
- The distancer can make a greater effort to share feelings, displaying vulnerability and helping the other partner to feel more connected.
- The couple can agree on ways to call time-out when the pursuer feels caught up in the blame game or the distancer feels invaded or overwhelmed.
- The couple can discuss the pursuer/distancer dynamic and discuss ways to break the cycle.

Active Listening

One of the observable laws of relationships is that *resistance breeds resistance.* If you argue with, contradict, or discount what your partner says, you will get the same resistance back in kind. Some of us think that if we just provide a few more facts, a few more arguments, we can make the other person see things our way. Instead we simply escalate the argument. Arguing with your partner's feelings communicates that either you're not willing to listen or you don't value your partner's emotions.

One cause of resistance is the belief that if we don't fix how the person is feeling, they will continue to feel that way forever. Nothing is further from the truth. When feelings are resisted, they stick around. The person will dig in and defend their feelings more strongly. When feelings are accepted, however, they begin to change. Sometimes, when their feelings are met with acceptance, people change a lot in a short time.

Many people, particularly men, feel that it is their job to find a solution for any feeling their partner may express. If the partner is unhappy, it is their job to fix it. Women are more inclined to share feelings without any expectation of a fix, gaining satisfaction from knowing that others know and understand how they feel.

These differences in expectations create a mismatch in communication. One reason men shy away from sharing feelings is they feel inadequate, because they fear they cannot come up with a solution — even though that's not what they are being asked to do.

One of the most valuable skills you can learn is *active listening*. This technique provides a way to accept feelings without either agreeing or disagreeing with them. It is designed to be supportive without being judgmental.

The goal in effective listening is acceptance, not agreement. There's a big difference between the two. Here's an example:

Agreement: "You're right, she should have consulted with you. I'd be upset too."

Acceptance: "So you're feeling hurt that Monica didn't consult with you."

Acceptance shows that you understand and accept that the other person feels the way they do. Agreement says that you approve of their feelings and would feel the same way.

With active listening, you are trying to understand the other person's reality even when your own reality is different. You don't necessarily want to agree with the other reality, which might be equivalent to giving up your own reality. But you do want the other person to know that you understand theirs.

Here's what happens in a typical conflict:

What Margaret says	What George says	What Margaret hears from George
Why do we have to be the ones to leave the party early?	You know I have to leave for work early tomorrow.	You're being thoughtless.
Well, it always seems like whenever we're having fun, we have to cut it short.	Well, we have to earn a living.	You're not being reasonable.
Just once in our lives I'd like to be able to have some fun without being reminded that we have to earn a living.	Get real! Earning a living is reality unless we win the lottery.	You're not being reasonable.
Well maybe it's time to shake things up. Why do we have to be so responsible all the time? Whatever happened to our vow to "live free"?	Well, we should have thought about that before we had kids. We have responsibilities now. We said we were going to put them first.	It's irresponsible to feel that way.

It would be easy for this discussion to turn into a fight. Margaret could easily attack George for suppressing anything fun, for being overly responsible. Margaret could be attacked for being irresponsible, unwilling to accept the consequences of decisions they made together. And on it would go.

Here's how the conversation might go if George uses active listening:

What Margaret says	What George says	What Margaret hears from George
Why do we have to be the ones to leave the party early?	You're disappointed we have to leave early.	I understand and accept how you feel.
Yeah, it seems like everything we do these days is being responsible. We never do anything fun unless it involves the kids.	So, it's not just the party. It seems like we're being super responsible all the time.	I understand and accept how you feel.
That's for sure. And I love the kids, and all, but I miss the times when you and I could have fun, without it always being about the kids.	You miss just having fun together, not always doing something focused on the kids.	I understand and accept how you feel.

What Margaret says	What George says	What Margaret hears from George
I remember when we'd say we were going to "live free." Whatever happened to those two kids who weren't going to live their whole lives by the conventions? I'd still like to have some of that in our lives.	It seems to you like we've forgotten who we wanted to be. Instead we're just following all the conventions.	I understand and accept how you feel.

This conversation would be ongoing. George likely has some of the same feelings. After talking about the issue, they may come up with some ideas for having fun but still accepting the responsibilities they accepted when they decided to have kids.

There are two things to notice about this version of the conversation. First, Margaret and George don't end up seeing each other as the problem. Second, Margaret felt free to share some of her deeper feelings.

The big shift in active listening is that the focus of attention is on the other person's feelings. The key principle is to respond by summarizing, in your own words, what you understand the other person is saying, and check in with the other person to see whether your understanding is accurate.

Active listening has been called by many different names, including *reflective listening*, *mirroring*, and *reframing*. I prefer the term *active listening* because it suggests that the listener has an active role in understanding the communication.

Here are more conversations showing the difference between typical listening and active listening:

Typical Listening

> **Regina:** I can't believe Jenny just went ahead and made a decision without consulting me.
>
> **Anthony:** She probably thought she was the one who had all the information about the situation, so it made sense for her to go ahead and make the decision.
>
> **Regina:** How come you are standing up for her? I'm your wife. You are supposed to be supportive of me.
>
> **Anthony:** I'm trying to be supportive, but I thought maybe you weren't seeing the whole picture.
>
> **Regina:** The whole picture! You jerk. I'm just as smart as you are, and I don't need you telling me how I should feel.

Active Listening

> **Regina:** I can't believe Jenny just went ahead and made a decision without consulting me.
>
> **Anthony** (using active listening): So you felt left out of the decision.
>
> **Regina:** You're darn right. I had some ideas about how to handle the situation.
>
> **Anthony:** You're feeling that your thoughts and feelings were ignored.

Regina: That's right. I want to be treated as an equal. When someone makes a decision like that, I want them to consult with me.

Anthony: When you aren't consulted, it doesn't feel like you are treated as an equal.

Regina: That's right. Being left out reminds me of my childhood. There's very little I wanted that I didn't get. But I was always treated as if I didn't have anything important to say.

Anthony: So when you're left out of decisions, it makes you feel like you are being treated as a child.

Regina: That's right.

Some of these responses may strike you as stiff, artificial, or even patronizing. I've had the same reaction when reading transcripts of real conversations like this. Yet I can testify that these responses, offered in a genuine and caring way, are often experienced as very supportive. Notice the number of times Regina says "That's right." Each one indicates that Regina feels that the listener understands her.

Furthermore, because the feelings she describes are being accepted, Regina feels free to explore new feelings, and in the process makes the discovery that her present feelings are linked to childhood experiences. She probably would never have had this insight if the listener had responded in a less accepting way.

Guidelines for Active Listening

There are four basic guidelines for becoming an effective active listener:

1. *Summarize, don't judge.*

The main message you want to communicate is acceptance. Most of us are far more skilled at being judgmental than being accepting: we even pronounce judgment on our own behavior. When we listen to our friends and loved ones, we too often judge them too.

When someone feels hurt or rejected, instead of acknowledging those feelings, we're likely to say something like "Oh, you shouldn't feel that way. I'm sure she didn't mean it," or even "Feeling sorry for yourself is not going to get you where you want to go." These responses end up being dismissive, telling the other person that it is not okay to feel the way they feel, even though we are trying to be reassuring or encouraging.

The premise of active listening is that it is okay for the speaker to feel whatever it is they feel. It is not the listener's job to decide whether they *should* feel that way but simply to summarize an understanding of what the other person does feel and think. The listener doesn't have to judge them or try to make them feel better, only to accept the way they feel right now.

2. *Summarize both feelings and ideas.*

People sometimes worry that active listening will make them sound like a parrot. There is some risk of that if you summarize only the factual ideas and content, and not the feelings. If someone says, "I'm so fed up, I don't want to attend that meeting," and you summarize by saying "You don't want to attend the meeting," their response might be "I just told you that."

But if you summarize both the feeling and the ideas — saying "You've just had it, and don't even want to attend the meeting" —

their response will likely be "That's right, I'm really tired of it." The stronger the feeling being expressed, the more important it is that you summarize the feeling part of the message. In fact, with really intense feelings, it is far more important to summarize the feelings than every single one of the ideas.

The one exception to being sure to capture strong feelings is when you are acting as a meeting leader or mediator. Then there may be many occasions when you want to summarize the ideas, and a summary of feelings may not be needed or may not be appropriate. Active listening is an extremely valuable skill for leading meetings or seeking agreement between multiple parties.

3. Reflect the intensity of the speaker's feelings.

Feelings come in all levels of intensity. Anger, for example, ranges all the way from irritation at one end of the scale to fury or rage at the other. An active-listening summary of feelings should reflect the intensity of the feelings being expressed. If someone is deeply upset by something, your response should include words like *outraged*, *infuriated*, and *furious*. If your choice of words does not reflect the intensity of the speaker's feelings, they will feel that you don't really accept their feelings.

It is also possible to overshoot by using words such as *upset*, *angry*, and *disturbed* for situations where people are only mildly concerned. Then they may feel "led," or patronized. The good news is that active listening is largely self-correcting. If your choice of feeling words is either too high or too low in intensity, the speaker will usually correct you by saying something like "I'm not just concerned, I'm really *upset*" or "It's not that big a deal. I'm a little worried, but…"

When you hear corrections like this, your next active-listening response needs to reflect the revised intensity: "So you are a lot more than just concerned, you're really upset that..." or "So you don't want to make too big a thing of it, but it still bothers you that..." As long as you acknowledge the mismatch in intensity, little harm is done.

4. Avoid lead-in phrases.

Some teachers of active listening advise using lead-in phrases like "I hear you saying..." or "If I understand you..." The intent of these phrases is to signal that the listener's summary may not be completely accurate: the information is being presented subject to the sender's acceptance. Although they are well-intentioned, lead-in phrases call attention to the listener, rather than keeping the focus on the sender. In effect they say, "Watch me do my listening thing."

You don't need lead-in phrases. Drop them. But you should approach the situation with humility. Not only may you come up with a summary that misses the mark, but if you start to think you know where the conversation is going, you may miss sudden detours and changes in direction.

If the sender corrects your active listening response, always accept the correction. There's nothing more inappropriate than a listener trying to defend their summary as correct when the speaker says it is not.

There Are Lots of Right Answers

When I teach active listening, I often find students trying to come up with the perfect response. The good news is that there are many right answers. The only real judge of your active listening response is the speaker. As long as the person keeps talking to you, and you keep reflecting any needed corrections, active listening is working.

What matters most is whether the speaker gets the message that you are listening and really want to understand. I've seen active listeners to whom speakers did not respond, even though they were very facile, because the speakers got the feeling that this was just a mechanical exercise. I've also seen people who were not very skilled at active listening receive high marks from speakers because the listeners conveyed a genuine desire to understand.

I do know, however, that active listening takes practice. I first learned the skill in order to be a better parent, but I found I needed to do it regularly before I could use it in really difficult circumstances. You may even want to agree to some practice sessions where you and your partner listen to each other and discuss how you are doing.

When to Use Active Listening

Some of the indicators that active listening is appropriate are the following:

- The speaker is expressing intense emotions.
- The speaker begins to repeat what they're saying, often with added emphasis.
- The speaker seems troubled by feelings.
- The speaker says, "You just don't understand..."

Active listening is useful when another person has feelings they need to talk about. If it's you who is upset or worried, then the appropriate skill is "I" messages (see chapter 6).

Active Listening in Close Relationships

Ironically, the hardest person to use active listening with is your partner, particularly if they are upset with you. Someone you love can stimulate your feelings faster than anyone else. Soon you may be unable to keep the focus on the other person's feelings. In addition, when two people are upset with each other, neither one wants the other person to play the role of helper or therapist. So active listening may come across as artificial, or distancing, even though both people are making a genuine effort to understand each other.

There's a paradox here. When people are in a fight, it would be helpful if they had their feelings acknowledged, which active listening can do. On the other hand, active listening may seem artificial, not the real you.

It may be time for the Five-Minute Rule.

The Five-Minute Rule

Active listening requires you to genuinely hear what the other person is saying. When I am doing active listening, I sometimes have the feeling that I need to clear out a space inside me, putting aside my own feelings, to be able to hear what the other person has to say. Sometimes it takes a real effort.

There will be times when active listening isn't possible for you: you may have so many feelings that you simply can't create space inside for the other person's feelings. This is particularly true if their feelings are about you. It is the rare person who can use active listening when they are the target of another person's anger or frustration.

Yet it remains true that resistance breeds resistance. If you give up on active listening and just fire back with your charges and countercharges, sharing feelings can quickly turn into a nasty fight. If you can't do active listening, but you know that resistance is likely to make things worse, what is the solution?

Years ago a marriage counselor taught my wife and me a simple technique that may have saved our marriage. It's called the Five-Minute Rule. Each person gets five minutes to say whatever they want, any way they want. The other person does not interrupt at all (or display any emphatic body language). Then they switch. The person who has been silent gets five minutes to say whatever they want, and the other person remains silent. If, at the end of both turns, people still have feelings they need to express, they do another round of five minutes each.

There are ground rules. Both people agree that either one can invoke the Five-Minute Rule at any time (with some possible exceptions, such as not in front of the children or other people). Once the Five-Minute Rule has been invoked, both people stop whatever they are doing. The only discussion that is allowed is who is going to speak first. Sometimes it is obvious that one of you has a more urgent need to express feelings. But if it's not obvious, flip a coin.

The reason the Five-Minute Rule works is that for five minutes nobody is telling you that you are bad, stupid, or crazy for feeling the way you do. In ordinary tit-for-tat arguments, you are being told you are wrong every twenty seconds or so. Five minutes is long enough that some of the heat of the argument dissipates. I find, for example, that after about four minutes I am repeating myself to the point where I'm beginning to bore even myself. I still feel the way I did, but a whole lot of the intensity has gone out of my feelings. I don't have the feeling that I just *have* to get the other person to understand and respond.

My wife and I have used the Five-Minute Rule many times, and it is a relationship saver. After a round or two, one or the other of us is willing to make some conciliatory gesture: "Well, I guess I could pick up more often." Sometimes the exchange ends with both of us simply saying, "I don't have anything more I need to say." That seems pretty anticlimactic, but it's actually a pretty good place from which to begin repairing the relationship. At other times, one of us is able to do some active listening.

When using the Five-Minute Rule, do not interrupt your partner, no matter how he or she is expressing feelings. If each of you can avoid blaming and accusing during your five minutes of speaking, it will make it easier to feel good about each other when the exchange is over. If you interrupt your partner to point out that he or she is doing a poor job of sending "I" messages, you will so antagonize them that you'll lose all the benefits of the Five-Minute Rule, or you'll trigger a whole different argument.

Above all, we want to avoid behaviors that make fights escalate to painful levels. If we can learn to identify behaviors that make things escalate, we can keep ourselves from engaging in them. That's the next step on our journey.

Summary

In relationships, resistance breeds resistance. If you argue with, contradict, or discount what your partner says, you will encounter the same resistance from them. When feelings are resisted, they stick around. When feelings are accepted, they begin to change, and people themselves can change a lot in a short period of time.

Active listening is a useful technique for enabling people to feel that their feelings are accepted and understood. The starting premise is that it is okay for the speaker to feel whatever it is they feel. The listener does not judge or comment but summarizes their understanding of what the other person feels and thinks.

When active listening isn't possible because both people are experiencing intense feelings that occupy all their attention, you can use techniques such as the Five-Minute Rule that give each of you a chance to express your feelings without contradiction or disagreement.

CHAPTER EIGHT

Avoiding Escalation

Learn to identify behaviors that cause fights
to escalate, and set mutually acceptable rules
to limit these behaviors.

Fights, particularly between couples, can start over the stupidest of things. Sadly, these silly little squabbles can escalate to the point that both people feel hurt, angry, and rejected. It's hard on the relationship and sometimes even leads to the end of the relationship. To prevent minor fights from becoming battles, we need to learn how to keep them from escalating.

Here's an example of a fight that escalates:

Dennis (husband who has just walked in the door at the end of a long day of work): Hey, what's this? The house is a mess, and you're just sitting watching soap operas on TV.

Theresa (wife): I've been going like crazy all day. This is the first chance I've had to rest. You try taking care of a three-year-old and a five-year-old. Who the hell do you think you are, just marching in and ordering me around?

Dennis: I'm someone who expects to come home to find you've done the chores you're responsible for. Instead I find you just lazing around. I'm busting my butt all day, and I come home to find you haven't done anything. It's not fair. I work hard, and I expect you to hold up your end of the bargain.

Theresa: No, what you expect is some kind of slave you can order around. You just want to be the lord and master, pushing me around.

Dennis: I don't want a slave. I just want someone who will do what she's supposed to do. Keeping the house clean is your job, and I expect you to do it, not just watch TV. It's like everything else. You just lie around and expect me to make things happen.

Theresa: Just lie around — you bastard! If you ever took an interest in the kids, you'd learn how much work it is to keep them from killing each other.

Dennis: You don't think I take an interest in the kids. I spend all kinds of time with the kids. But I have to work eight to ten hours a day, plus usually Saturday. So I'm counting on you to carry your share of the load. But no, you'd rather just sit and watch TV.

Theresa: Are you calling me lazy? You jerk! You're always spending weekends watching football games on TV, and evenings you mostly just stomp around the place telling the kids to shut up. No wonder they don't even want to be around you much anymore.

Dennis: You lazy slut. Everybody in the neighborhood knows you're lazy. The guys even talk about it.

Theresa: Well, all the women in the neighborhood call
you a pompous ass, always ordering everybody
around and pretending you know everything. They're
all sorry for me just being married to you. Well, I've
had it. I quit. You can just fix your own damn dinner.

Dennis: Well, screw you. I'm going out. Who wants to be
around such an irresponsible bitch? (*Slams the door
on the way out*)

Fights like this don't just escalate on their own: they escalate
because of the behaviors in which we, and our partners, engage.
And escalation has a predictable pattern.

Escalation is triggered when someone feels poked, threatened,
or put down. Again, the initial incident may be something very
small. The first escalating behavior is almost always blaming and
accusing. This typically involves a lot of "you" messages: "You did
this," "You did that." Dennis and Theresa's exchange is all blame
and accusation, from the first words out of Dennis's mouth.

Blaming and accusing often lead to the second stage of escalation, which is name-calling. In addition to calling her lazy, Dennis
calls Theresa a slut and an irresponsible bitch. Theresa calls Dennis a bastard, a jerk, and a pompous ass.

What happens next is that both parties expand the issue about
which they are fighting. For example, a gripe about leaving the
cap off the toothpaste might lead to "You're always so messy" and
then to "You just don't take responsibility for anything, except
maybe for your stupid truck." It might escalate to remarks like
"Your mother feels the same way about you" and "I don't know
why I ever married someone so irresponsible." An argument that
begins with the toothpaste cap moves to the partner's total irre-
sponsibility and even to questioning their suitability as a partner.

In an effort to strengthen their position, both people may start to claim allies, bolstering their position by claiming the support of others. Dennis says, "Everybody in the neighborhood knows you're lazy." Theresa retorts, "Well, all the women in the neighborhood call you a pompous ass." Sometimes both people actively enlist the people around them to be on their side. This can lead to long-lasting family feuds. In the worst case, parents may try to get their kids on their side, putting the kids in the position of having to choose between parents.

As the fight escalates, both sides often resort to exaggeration, sweeping generalizations, character attacks, and prolonged and hostile periods of silence. You can tell you've reached this stage when you, or your partner, is saying "You always..." or "You never..." Sometimes people even cut off direct communication, sending messages through other people: "Johnny, tell your father that he has to cut the lawn."

As the escalation occurs, both people start to take positions that are rigid or extreme. You might not have cared that much to start with, but now you find yourself becoming very rigid: "I'll never do that." If the fight escalates far enough, the goal simply becomes to hurt the other person verbally or even physically. If this goes on for long, the relationship may be destroyed. To stop this pattern of escalation, we have to learn to recognize behaviors that cause it and stop engaging in them.

In any relationship there are three parties: Me, You, and We. When fights escalate, we lose track of and sometimes even destroy the We. This leads to a kind of First Commandment for handling conflicts in a relationship:

Protect your relationship even when you are in conflict.

Even while you are fighting, remember that there is a We that may be fragile but incredibly valuable, and avoid behaviors that threaten the We.

We threaten the We because four things happen during escalation:

- We start seeing the other person as an adversary, or the enemy.
- We lose touch with the fact that we love the other person. We may have been very loving just an hour ago. But right now we hate their guts.
- During escalation, both partners become less willing to listen.
- We become less willing to expose our deeper feelings and sometimes suspend communication altogether.

Each person is justifying their own behavior as getting even for what the other person said or did. He feels resentful because his partner blamed him unfairly, so he feels justified in calling her a nasty name. She is mad about his name-calling, so she feels justified in expanding the issue, and so on. In reality, this really means that neither person is taking responsibility for their own behavior. Everything they say is based on getting even.

Rules of Engagement

This chapter presents some rules of engagement that will help you avoid behaviors that escalate fights. Obviously, it's better if both people play by these rules, so I encourage you to discuss these rules with your partner and see if you can reach an agreement on at least some of them.

Even if you and your partner can't agree, though, follow these rules yourself. Take responsibility for your own behavior, regardless of what your partner does. If you want to change the usual outcome, you have to start by changing your behavior.

Rule 1. Avoid blaming and accusing. Express feelings using "I" messages.

Rule 2. Don't engage in name-calling or labeling. Describe the other person's behavior, and how it makes you feel, without judging or evaluating it.

Rule 3. Don't expand the issue. Don't pile on with additional issues, and, in particular, don't make the issue bigger.

Rule 4. Don't use other people or authorities as ammunition. Trying to get more power by claiming the support of others will just result in the other person's trying to top that.

Rule 5. Avoid sweeping generalizations like "You always" or "You never." This kind of generalization is always untrue and will always stimulate powerful counterattacks.

Rule 6. Do whatever you can to break the patterns of resistance. Communicate your feelings, but don't try to prove you are right. Acknowledge things you've done that were thoughtless or bad. Support ideas suggested by the other person. It's sometimes hard to avoid defensiveness, particularly when you feel like you are under attack. But defensiveness is not effective in countering the attack. It just breeds defensiveness in the other person. Sometimes we are unaware that we are being defensive. Part of avoiding defensiveness is becoming aware of it when we do it.

Rule 7. If you're dealing with a practical problem, don't mix the conflict phase with the problem-solving phase. Resolve the emotional dispute first, then set a later date to wrestle with practical problem-solving (the next chapter describes a process for this). Otherwise the bad feelings from the dispute will poison the problem-solving.

Summary

Fights don't escalate on their own: they escalate because of the behaviors in which we engage. The typical pattern of escalation involves blaming and accusing, followed by name-calling. Next, both parties expand the issue about which they are fighting. Both people may then start to bolster their position by claiming the support of others. The next stage is distortion of communication, including exaggeration, sweeping generalizations, character attacks, and hostile silence. Eventually, the goal simply becomes to hurt each other verbally or sometimes even physically. If this goes on for long, the relationship may be destroyed.

In any relationship there are three parties: Me, You, and We. Even while you are fighting, avoid behaviors that threaten the We.

CHAPTER NINE

Collaborative Problem-Solving

Use a problem-solving process that says
"*We* have a problem," not "*You* are the problem."

It takes time to change your emotional reality. After all, both you and your partner have years invested in your old ways of viewing reality. Meantime, life goes on, and you must solve real problems despite continuing differences in your emotional realities.

Often everyday problems are difficult to solve because they involve differences in emotional reality. Take the case of Rex and Maria.

Rex and Maria have a transportation problem. Recently some expensive repairs on their truck have raised the issue of whether there is a better solution to the family's transportation needs.

Both Rex and Maria work, but their combined income is still modest, particularly with the expenses for their children, Johnny (age seven) and Gloria (age nine). In addition to normal expenses, each of the children has outside interests that cost money. Gloria takes weekly piano lessons and is showing some real aptitude. Johnny loves all sports and is constantly in need of sporting equipment.

Most of the possible solutions would require everybody — including the kids — to scrimp a bit. Rex and Maria have tried to discuss the problem, but each time they've gotten into an argument. Once it ended up in a fight about what was fair. Maria feels the current situation in unfair: Rex can go anywhere he wants in the truck, while Maria is stuck taking the bus.

Another time, the couple ended up arguing about how much money they should spend on the kids' activities. Maria believes it is their responsibility to give their kids opportunities they themselves didn't have. She was raised in a family where everybody had to do without. When she was young, she vowed that her own children would get whatever they needed, even if she or her husband had to do without. Rex's family was a bit more comfortable financially. They had to do without occasionally, but Rex doesn't remember any real hardship.

This issue turned into a nasty argument. When Rex accused Maria of being unrealistic, saying that the kids could do without things occasionally, Maria felt that some of her fundamental beliefs about what parents should give children were in danger of being violated.

Rex and Maria have very different emotional realities about providing for their children. Maria feels very deeply that the kids should not have to do without. Rex feels they are teaching their kids false values if they never have to make do.

There's also a clash between their emotional realities regarding who makes decisions. Rex comes from a family where transportation was considered the man's responsibility, so he assumes that he makes the decisions. Maria feels left out and believes they should be equal partners in decision-making.

The problem is further complicated by Maria's feeling that the current situation is unfair. She suffers through the daily bus ride, while everybody else in the family gets prompt transportation. How do Rex and Maria solve this problem?

Relationship Issues

First of all, whenever people work together to solve a problem, they engage with questions of both content — issues such as how they are going to get to work and handle monthly bills — and relationship — how much does each person feel valued or accepted?

Relationship is often communicated by *how* decisions are made — by the process rather than the outcome. People learn they are equal when they feel they have an equal say in the decision-making process.

For generations parents have helped two children split the last piece of cake fairly by stipulating that one child cuts the cake, and the other is the first to choose a piece. This process usually guarantees that the pieces of cake are exactly equal. It not only teaches children how to split the cake but also lets the parent communicate important values:

- I love you both equally.
- You are to treat each other as equals.
- You are to treat each other with respect.

Processes communicate values, and these values can change people's behavior. When people feel valued, they can consider a range of solutions. When they don't feel valued, they tend to oppose solutions.

In Rex and Maria's household, Maria doesn't feel valued. She has to take the bus while everybody else in the family has a ride.

The issue can be resolved only if the problem-solving process communicates to Maria that she is valued, an equal. Addressing this relationship issue is at least as important as the details of their transportation problem.

Even though Rex was raised in a family where the men made all the decisions about transportation — on the basis that they knew more about cars — Rex is willing to concede that he and Maria should both be involved in transportation decision-making. But he forgets sometimes. His head says they should be equal, but his habit is to just go ahead and make decisions.

Dealing with Different Emotional Realities

The second challenge in solving Rex and Maria's transportation problem is the difference in their views about what they owe their children. Without some resolution of these differing emotional realities, any alternative that requires the children to give up anything in order to reduce household costs may not be acceptable to Maria.

Of all the ways to address differing emotional realities, none is as important as the approach the couple takes when they try to solve problems. If Rex and Maria see each other as the obstacle to solving the problem, their chances of finding a solution acceptable to both of them will be sorely limited. If they can operate from the position that "*we* have a problem," they can consider a greater range of alternatives.

A Collaborative Problem-Solving Process

Below I describe a process that couples can use to address problems. It is simply the best and simplest process I know of. It works. I learned the basics of it from Dr. Tom Gordon, and since then

I've taught this process to hundreds of couples as well as to scores of companies and agencies. Others have taught the same or similar processes.

Like every process, this one is based on values. It assumes, for example, that the decision-makers are equals. It provides a common language and structure that both simplify and reduce the number of arguments over how to approach the problem.

Here are the basic steps in collaborative problem-solving:

1. Agree on what all parties need for the issue to be resolved.

Some years ago my wife and I were in a Central European country teaching conflict-resolution skills. This country was engaged in a major dispute with a breakaway province, with conflicts involving issues of ethnicity and religion. Roger Fisher, the coauthor of *Getting to Yes*, and a renowned expert on negotiation, happened to be in town as well. Fisher was asked by several government officials whether he could help them with negotiations. His response was: "As soon as you understand the other group's concerns as well as your own, I can help."

This is an equally good principle for couples. The first step in problem-solving is to develop a shared and thorough understanding of what each person needs. This means both people need to understand both the content issues and the relationship issues underlying the disagreement. If the issue affects other parties, such as children, you need to understand their content and relationship issues as well. You'll need to use both "I" messages and active listening, discussed in chapters 6 and 7, to do your best possible job of understanding the problem.

You might even want to write down your understanding of the needs that must be addressed for the problem to be solved. The table below outlines the needs in Rex and Maria's household:

	Rex's concerns	Maria's concerns	Kids' concerns
Content	Worried about cost of future repairs for truck Sometimes needs truck to haul materials to work	Hates bus ride Worried about cost of future repairs for truck	Want to keep what they have now
Relationship	Used to being the person who makes decisions about issues like transportation Enjoys peer approval when he drives truck to work	Feels she gets the worst of the deal by having to take the bus Feels she's been excluded from earlier decision-making about transportation Believes kids should not have to do without	Like to be consulted on issues that affect them

Strangely, most people — whether in intimate relationships or in business — skip over this problem-definition stage and also often ignore relationship issues entirely. Instead they jump straight to proposing solutions. As a result, they often adopt solutions to the wrong problem or can't understand why other people oppose their solution.

In my experience, it's productive to spend 50 percent or more of the available problem-solving time on defining the problem.

2. Brainstorm a list of alternative solutions.

The next step is to brainstorm a list of alternative solutions. *Brainstorming* refers to a very specific process: the affected parties propose as many possible solutions as they can think of, without judgment or evaluation.

There are some very important principles underlying brainstorming:

- People can be most creative when they feel safe psychologically. If every idea is judged when it is suggested, they will tend to shut down. Do *not* evaluate the possible solutions during brainstorming. Just write them down without comment.
- Goofy-sounding ideas often lead to creative breakthroughs. The goofy idea may not, in itself, have value, but it may loosen up your thinking enough to lead to solutions you would never have thought of otherwise.
- Go for quantity. Research on brainstorming shows that groups that generate lots of solutions are more likely to come up with creative solutions than groups that generate just a few. The creative solutions usually come *after* the obvious solutions have been listed.

- Get everybody engaged in generating multiple solutions. One of the obstacles to reaching a solution that everyone agrees to is the situation where each person digs in and defends their own preferred solution. But if Rex and Maria have each generated five to ten possible solutions, neither of them has the same emotional commitment to "their" solution.
- Often the solution that is finally agreed on is based on one person's thinking stimulated by someone else's idea. Combine possible solutions. Piggyback on each other's ideas.

3. Agree on which solution(s) best meet(s) all parties' needs.

After brainstorming solutions, you can evaluate them all to your heart's content. But here's where the time you spent clarifying everybody's needs pays off. The standard against which you evaluate solutions is your list of everyone's needs — both content and relationship needs. Which solution does the best job of meeting all those needs? Remember to use "I" messages to describe how a possible solution affects you. Use active listening to respond to others' concerns or thinking.

4. Agree on how to implement the solution.

I've seen couples do a great job on steps 1–3, then end up angry and resentful because they didn't fully discuss how their solution was going to be implemented. One couple agreed on the need to buy a new car but almost divorced when the husband went out and bought a new car without consulting his wife on selecting it.

Develop a clear plan for who is going to do what and when. Be sure to specify which of you is responsible for each step.

Often having joint responsibility means that no one truly feels responsible.

5. Agree on a way to determine whether the solution is working.

There's a tendency, once a solution has been agreed on, to assume the problem is solved. But in real life, some well-intentioned solutions don't work, and another crisis ensues when people recognize that their solution isn't working. Agree on how and when you will jointly assess whether your chosen solution is doing the job.

If it isn't working, go through the process again, trying to define clearly the reasons why it is not working. Above all, be sure to maintain the approach of "*we* have a problem" rather than blaming each other for why the first solution didn't work.

When I use the example of Maria and Rex in some of my training courses, participants have come up with some off-the-wall solutions, but most solutions involve some variation of selling the truck, buying two inexpensive cars, and getting some savings from having Johnny get by with used athletic equipment and cutting back a bit on Gloria's music lessons. One group, I remember, suggested that when Maria got a car she should quit her job and become an Uber driver.

Whether any savings can be derived from cutting back on the kids' activities depends on Maria. She is the one who wants to be sure the kids have everything they need. Perhaps by participating in the decision she can be comfortable with the accommodation reached.

How the kids react to the changes may be even more important. They should be included in the discussion. If the problem is presented to them as "We need to save money to buy a car so Mom doesn't have to take the bus," they may have suggestions, or may be more willing to accept changes. If person A and person B get together and collaboratively agree upon what person C should do, there's no guarantee that person C will buy into that agreement.

Summary

The essential principle in problem-solving for couples is to take the approach that "*we* have a problem," rather than seeing their partner as the barrier to solving the problem. When people feel valued, they are more open to considering alternative solutions. An effective problem-solving process identifies each party's needs, brainstorms solutions, arrives at a solution, and includes a process for deciding whether the solution is working.

PART THREE

TOOLS
and
APPROACHES

CHAPTER TEN

Conflicts over Values

*Look for the positive good that your
partner supports, even when your partner opposes
what you think is important.*

All of us must make hard decisions in life. These hard decisions demonstrate our *values*: the rules by which we decide what is good or bad, right or wrong, fair or unfair, rational or irrational.

Values include our judgments of the ends that really matter in life, such as freedom, happiness, equality, security, salvation, and enlightenment. Other values include the means — the qualities that may help us achieve those ends — such as being helpful, creative, elegant, polite, and cheerful. Finally, there are values relating to the processes by which we pursue our goals, such as openness, fairness, and efficiency.

These values shape our emotional realities, and our emotional realities in turn shape our values. The two are intertwined.

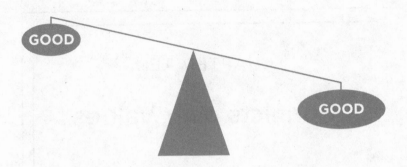

Things we think of as good are often in tension with other things we think are good. We want our children to be safe, but we also want them to have freedom. Complete freedom can endanger safety. Complete safety usually rules out complete freedom.

Most difficult decisions are actually choices about the relative weight or importance that should be given to two different values. Decisions that require weighing different social goods are called *values choices*. For example, in the United States we are currently debating how to balance national security with individual privacy. Both values are good. Which is more important in a particular situation is a matter of judgment. Another example is the use of seat belts in cars, a choice that balances comfort and convenience with safety. A government considering the mandatory use of seat belts is making a values choice between individual freedom and public safety.

All these values are good, desirable, and positive. No one opposes them. The issue is which values should prevail in a given situation.

Many of the conflicts between couples involve values choices. Our preferred course of action shows which values are most important to us in this situation. Each choice represents a balance between two goods.

When we confront someone with an emotional reality based on values that are substantially different from ours, the rules by which each of us judges reality come into conflict. We usually cope with this threat to our definition of reality by judging others to be ill-informed or to have evil motives. An educational program that one individual views as an outstanding program to encourage discipline may be seen by another as cruel and abusive. The two people's values are so different that they literally don't make any sense to each other.

When couples argue about what action to take, each frequently sees their partner as an opponent, someone who is against what they believe to be right. Your partner may oppose an action you think is important because it doesn't support their own view of what is good. Your partner's opposition is based on positive support for a value that they consider even more important. You are actually both defending what you view as a positive good.

One of the characteristics of values arguments is that each of you may see your "opponent" as overemotional and irrational, committed to premises that can't be justified rationally.

When You and Your Partner Have Different Values

The key to dealing with values differences is this: *even when your partner opposes what you think is important, look for the positive good that your partner supports.* Values choices are not black-and-white choices. They are usually a matter of finding a balance: recognizing that you both support a positive value, honoring both values to an extent, but perhaps giving greater weight to one of the values in particular circumstances. Your children's safety is good, but so is freedom of action. Which is more important in a given situation?

Your job as a couple is to identify the values for which each of you is arguing. When you recognize what the other person stands for, you may find that you are not so far apart. Even when you think a certain value — say, safety — is more important in a particular situation, you may acknowledge that comfort is important too. Instead of *either/or*, you are looking for *both/and*. You are working together to find ways to give both values a reasonable weight.

Identifying Values

Values are often implied in speech or behavior rather than explicitly stated. While they play a strong role in shaping our lives, when they are stated explicitly they often sound like symbols or abstractions, like "motherhood" or "apple pie," and are difficult to defend except as an act of faith. (Even the writers of the Declaration of Independence faced this difficulty: seeking to justify values as fundamental as "Life, Liberty, and the Pursuit of Happiness," they fell back on the phrase "We hold these truths to be self-evident.")

Think of identifying values as a puzzle you can solve together. Here are three indicators of implied values:

1. **Use of values-laden language.** Phrases we use to argue against certain choices, such as "throwing away our money," "coddling the kids," and "letting our parents run our lives," contain implied value judgments rather than directly stated ones. The values might be thrift, discipline, and freedom.

2. **Predicting a dire consequence.** When people fear that a course of action runs against a deeply held value, they often predict that it will result in some dire outcome. For

example, one parent might say: "You are spoiling the children by giving them everything they want." The fear is that the kids will turn out bad because they are unable to exercise self-discipline. In other circumstances, a partner might express a fear that you will end up bankrupt or that they'll never make friends.

It doesn't really matter whether the other person's fear makes any sense to you. I have a friend whose husband was deeply influenced by his parents' experiences during the Great Depression and food shortages during World War II. No amount of money will help him feel secure. That insecurity is one of his emotional realities. His wife has had to make peace with this. When they disagree, she tries to remember that what drives him is a desire for financial security, a value she also supports.

3. **Referring to a venerable source.** In defending their views, people may quote the Bible, the president, the latest self-help book, or someone they talked to at work. The strategy is to quote a source that the other person won't dare to challenge for fear of discrediting themselves. The difficulty is that sources that are venerated by one person may appear downright disreputable to another (like "that financial advice program on TV").

One way to approach a difference in values choices is for each person to list the values they think are particularly important in a given situation. Then you can ask whether there are any possible actions that would incorporate both values.

Chapter 9 describes a problem-solving process that may be useful in arriving at a solution you can both live with.

Summary

Values choices are essentially choices between two or more *positive goods*. Our choices of action illustrate our beliefs about which values are most important in a given situation. When another person has an emotional reality based on values substantially different from ours, the rules by which each of us judges reality may come into conflict. When this happens, couples frequently see each other as opposing what they believe to be right. But each person is actually defending what they view as a positive good. The key principle for dealing with values differences is this: *even when your partner opposes what you think is important, look for the positive good that your partner supports.*

CHAPTER ELEVEN

Reframing

Seek out new ways of perceiving reality
you can both agree on.

Mark Twain's fictional hero Tom Sawyer was highly skilled at reframing a situation. When Sawyer was forced to spend a holiday whitewashing a fence, his friends teased him because he had to work while they could play. He turned the tables on his friends, however, by redefining the task: "Does a boy get a chance to whitewash a fence every day?" Soon his friends were paying him for the privilege of doing the job.

We don't deal only with facts. We interpret the facts, and we interpret the facts within a context created by the way we "frame" the situation. The frame is the underlying beliefs and assumptions on which we base our interpretations. Tom Sawyer's friends started out with the frame that whitewashing the fence was an unpleasant task. Tom convinced them it was an honor and a privilege that they were willing to pay for.

Ordinarily, acting based on unconscious framing of situations is valuable and saves time. But old ways of framing our experiences may be locking us into unnecessary constraints. These old frames can prevent us from exploring and using our own abilities to our best advantage. They may even be responsible for an impasse between you and your partner over alternative realities. Reframing — shifting the perspective from which we experience and interpret a situation — can enable us to respond differently.

Every now and then John goes on a fishing trip with some old friends. When he returns from the trip, his wife, Ruth, asks him a whole lot of questions about what happened on the trip. John hates the questions, believing that she is checking up on him. He quickly becomes resentful and defensive, feeling that he has done nothing to justify suspicion, and they almost always get into a fight. John is almost ready to give up his fishing trips because they aren't worth the fight afterward. But then he resents the idea of being coerced into giving them up.

John interprets Ruth's questioning entirely in the context of what he sees as her jealousy and suspicion. He doesn't realize that he contributes to the communication problems through the angry and resentful way he responds to her questions. Given that Ruth, for her part, seems unable to skip the questions, there seems to be no way of escaping a hurtful fight.

Can John reframe the interaction? What if he framed Ruth's questions as a sign that she is feeling insecure and wants to know where she stands with him? Certainly if that were true, the appropriate response from John would be to act loving and reassuring. If he can change his behavior in this way, they may have a happy coming together, rather than a fight.

Stephen Covey, in his bestselling book *The Seven Habits of Highly Effective People*, describes an experience of sudden reframing:

I remember a mini–paradigm shift I experienced one Sunday morning on a subway in New York. People were sitting quietly — some reading newspapers, some lost in thought, some resting with their eyes closed. It was a calm, peaceful scene.

Then suddenly, a man and his children entered the subway car. The children were so loud and rambunctious that instantly the whole climate changed. The man sat down next to me and closed his eyes, apparently oblivious to the situation. The children were yelling back and forth, throwing things, even grabbing people's papers. It was very disturbing. And yet, the man sitting next to me did nothing.

It was difficult not to feel irritated. I could not believe that he could be so insensitive as to let his children run wild like that and do nothing about it, taking no responsibility at all. It was easy to see that everyone else on the subway felt irritated, too. So finally, with what I felt was unusual patience and restraint, I turned to him and said, "Sir, your children are really disturbing a lot of people. I wonder if you couldn't control them a little more?"

The man lifted his gaze as if to come to a consciousness of the situation for the first time and said softly, "Oh, you're right. I guess I should do something about it. We just came from the hospital where their mother died about an hour ago. I don't know what to think, and I guess they don't know how to handle it either.".…

Suddenly I saw things differently.…I behaved differently. My irritation vanished. I didn't have to worry about controlling my attitude or my behavior; my heart was filled with the man's pain. Feelings of sympathy and compassion flowed freely....Everything changed in an instant.

As this example shows, when the same "facts" are viewed in a different frame, the facts themselves may seem to change. Another example is how we might interpret someone's unwillingness to donate money to a local charity: we can see it as either stingy or thrifty, depending on our frame of reference. If you are facing a long, potentially boring automobile trip with a friend, you might reframe it as a splendid opportunity to get to know your friend even better.

If you and your partner have a continuing struggle because your emotional reality frames situations in a way that makes your partner's position seem unacceptable, you may be able to break the impasse by reframing the situation, finding other ways of understanding the situation that can accommodate both people's emotional realities.

Criteria for Reframing

We make meaning in the world around us by taking a limited number of external facts and interpreting them. Our interpretations are based on the frames of personal experience, the roles we play, and family dynamics.

When we talk about reframing, we're not talking about conning ourselves into a new interpretation or lying to ourselves. But what if there is an alternative set of meanings that explains the current situation as plausibly as the meanings that we've always used in the past? What if seeing someone as thrifty is at least as valid an interpretation as seeing them as stingy? A principal criterion for evaluating a new frame is that the new frame must offer at least as good an interpretation of the facts as the old frame. It must be equally believable, or more so.

Reframing can be used to break an emotional impasse either within yourself or with another person. Examining different values choices, as illustrated in chapter 10, involves some reframing: you reframe your partner's position when you look for the positive value your partner supports, rather than their apparent opposition to your values. You may want your children to be free to go out by themselves, for example, but your husband is opposed to the idea. Reframing starts by recognizing that he is concerned about their safety — something you support as well — rather than assuming that he opposes personal freedom. Recognizing that each of you is supporting a positive value — both personal freedom and security are good — reframes the argument.

Simply arguing that someone should reframe their views is unlikely to be successful. People who have a firm frame of reference are likely to dismiss or filter out alternative framings. The new frame must make sense to them: it has to be consistent with the facts and must fit into their overall approach to life. If there has been pain and hurt, the new frame must account for and acknowledge that pain. If you are working together as a couple, the discussion may sound like this: "You see it that way, and I see it this way....Let's find a way to make this work for both of us."

Reframing in Action

One way to see reframing in action is to notice how people reframe past experiences. Professionally successful people often report life experiences that completely disrupted their expected career path. Later they may say that the disruption "was the best thing that happened to me" and go on to explain how their current success could not have happened without the disruption of their earlier plans. They may acknowledge that at the time, it was hard for them to frame the event as anything but a failure or extremely damaging.

We may look back on experiences that at the time were horribly embarrassing — such as first dates, personal hygiene problems, or awkward meetings — and now see them as cute. But they sure didn't seem cute at the time. Now that we have survived these dreadful experiences, we can see them differently.

REFRAMING A "WEAKNESS" AS A STRENGTH

Reframing can be used not only to change our perspective of events or experiences, but also to change our negative judgments of qualities in ourselves or other people and see them in ways that are affirming. Here are some examples.

- **Passive** — able to accept things as they are
- **Submissive** — seeking authority and direction for one's actions; cautious
- **Seductive** — wanting to attract other people and be liked; needing a lot of attention
- **Oversensitive** — tuned in to other people; very alive and aware
- **Oppositional** — searching for one's own way of doing things; thinking independently
- **Self-deprecating** — able to acknowledge faults; humble

- **Prone to crying** — able to express emotion, especially hurt or anger; deeply caring
- **Rigid** — steadfast in purpose and beliefs; articulating clear boundaries
- **Hostile** — highly involved; high-energy
- **Confused** — in the process of breaking down old structures in preparation for new growth
- **Lazy** — laid back, mellow, relaxed, taking it easy; low-energy
- **Nagging** — concerned; trying to bring out the best in someone; really invested in getting things done

Closer to home, many teenage children see their parents as mean, overcontrolling, and a barrier to being accepted by their peers. Eventually these individuals may come to view their parents as loving and protective, but this reframing rarely occurs during their teens. It's more likely to occur when they become parents themselves.

The challenge is to reframe the experience while you are going through it, to free up more options or release tied-up energy.

Here are a few strategies for doing that:

- Brainstorm at least three possible reasons this situation could have arisen, in addition to the explanation you've been assuming.
- Reframe a problem as an opportunity.
- Reframe a weakness as a strength (see section above).
- Reframe an impossibility as a distant possibility.
- Define the situation as neutral ("I'm not an important

player in the situation") instead of oppressive ("They're out to get me").

- Ask how someone you revere (such as Jesus, Gandhi, or Martin Luther King) would solve this problem.
- Change the context: "Questioning everything is a problem for Joe now, but when he reaches adulthood it will be a strength."

I had an important experience with reframing early in my career. I had the opportunity to work closely for several years with a very distinguished man who became an important mentor to me. The relationship ended when he engaged in several behaviors that I found very hurtful. I chewed on that hurt periodically for a couple of years. Finally I asked myself, "How did he perceive the behaviors in which I engaged?" To my chagrin, I realized that there were several things I had done that he could have interpreted as disloyal or unsupportive. I still didn't see what I had done as justifying the destruction of the relationship, but once I understood how I had contributed to the situation, I was able almost immediately to stop grinding emotionally on the events. I changed my understanding of the situation by changing the frame to take his perceptions into account.

Reframing as Therapy

Psychotherapists use reframing extensively to help people resolve issues they find troubling. As the psychotherapist Mark Tyrrell puts it: "When someone is stuck in a particular thinking style and unconsciously assumes that their (limited, negative) view is the only perspective, then a major shift can occur when another wider, more flexible, and positive view is unexpectedly and unarguably demonstrated to them. After such a reframe moment, it is usually impossible for them to maintain the problem behavior in the same old limiting way." Here are some examples of approaches to reframing, reported by Tyrrell.

A newly qualified teacher was losing her confidence as a result of continual criticism from an older teacher. To help her avoid taking on the criticism as part of her identity, the therapist used a digestion metaphor and talked about some of the criticism as having "limited nutritional value." The teacher was also reminded that she could chew on the criticism for a while, and if she didn't like it, she could spit it out.

An individual was in danger of losing his job because of his angry outbursts and browbeating of employees. When asked, he reported that his greatest fear was that people would take advantage of him. A therapist asked him, "So how much longer are you going to let that anger take advantage of you?" In other words, the situation was reframed so that it became apparent to the client that it was his own anger, not the performance of his employees, that was undermining him.

Learning How to Reframe

Working with a therapist can be extremely helpful in reframing problematic situations. But many people do not have the time or money to work with a therapist. Here are some things you can do that may help you reframe a situation.

Journaling

Many people have found it helpful to maintain a journal, a summary of daily events with a particular emphasis on how you feel about those events. This journal can include the time of the mood or thought, the source of it, the extent or intensity, and how you responded to it, among other factors. Often when you go back and read past journal entries, your frame of reference becomes very visible. This may give you insights into what needs to change.

Thinking the Script through to the End

In your imagination, push the situation to its logical conclusion. What's the worst thing that could happen? Will you lose your job, marriage, or savings? How would you cope if these events occurred? What would you do? What could you do?

Most of the time when you predict the worst possible outcome, you'll find you're still standing at the end of it. Somehow, facing the worst reduces significantly the fear and anxiety associated with that possibility. It may be unpleasant, but you'll survive. Having looked at the worst-case scenario, you are free to get on with living. If it does happen, you are prepared for it.

Reframing Exercise

Here's an exercise you might use to help you reframe a difficult situation:

1. Identify the frame: the attitude or belief that is limiting your options, such as a fear of speaking in public.
2. Find the positive purpose or intention behind the frame. For example, avoiding public speaking protects you from criticism or ridicule.
3. Identify three other ways to satisfy that positive purpose that do not have the negative consequences of the original frame. Here are some examples:

- I've really blown some presentations, mostly when I didn't prepare well. But I'm also capable of being an effective speaker.
- I need more experience and training at public speaking, and I'm going to get it.
- I don't really know what I'm capable of.

4. Have the part of yourself that argues on behalf of the old frame agree to consider the three new frames.

5. Look for experiences you've had that support any of the three other frames.

6. Check in: Does any other part of yourself object to the choices?

7. Continue to look for experiences that support the new frame. Begin to build a new narrative about your attitude toward public speaking.

What would happen if we reframed the biggest frame of all — our life story? If we understood our life story differently, would life be different for us now? That's the subject for the next chapter.

Summary

We interpret external facts within a frame structured by our underlying beliefs and assumptions. You may be able to break an impasse with yourself or your partner by reframing the situation: finding alternative ways of understanding the situation that can explain it just as well as your original understanding and can accommodate different emotional realities. Techniques such as journaling, envisioning possible outcomes, and reframing exercises can help with the process.

CHAPTER TWELVE

Reframing Your Life Story

Reframe your life story as needed
to create options and free up capabilities.

When you tell your life story, you make choices about the events and incidents you include. These choices reveal the frame through which you view your life. If you view yourself as shy and needing protection, you may, in fact, have left out situations in which you acted assertively and bravely.

One way to change your life is to change your life story. By looking for events that tell a different story, you may be able to change your frame of reference, reclaim parts of yourself, and see yourself in a different light. Some of those other events, the ones you didn't include, might create an entirely different frame for your life.

According to Jill Freedman and Gene Combs, leaders in the field of narrative therapy, "In any life there are always more events that don't get 'storied' than there are ones that do — even the longest and most complex autobiography leaves out more than it includes. This means that when life narratives carry hurtful meanings or seem to offer only unpleasant choices, they can be changed by highlighting different, previously un-storied events or by taking new meaning from already-storied events, thereby constructing new narratives." The motto for this process might well be "It's not always like this."

Fredrico saw himself as a weak person, often unable to stand up for himself. When asked to go back over his life and remember situations where he successfully stood up for himself, he was startled to find quite a number of such experiences. Having recalled them, he could begin to look at what was different about the situations in which he was able to defend himself and those in which he felt vulnerable. Soon he began to see himself as stronger, able to protect his own interests, and more aware of what circumstances made him feel passive. He was beginning to change his story to one that he liked much better. From that point, it was his job to strengthen the new story and extend it into the future.

Making a Choice about Life Narratives

I have learned from experience that it is possible to choose which experiences to include in my own life story.

When I was about four years old, I was put in a crib to take a nap while my mother also grabbed a badly needed nap. To keep me from getting too restless, in case I woke up before she did, she gave me an old necklace to play with. Naturally I woke up first, but I played quietly with the necklace for some time. Then the worn-out cord broke, and the beads from the necklace scattered across the floor, waking my mother. She was unusually distraught and upset with me. (I later learned that the necklace had been given to her by a childhood sweetheart.) My conclusion from the experience was that there was no chance of winning. Even when I'd behaved well and done everything asked of me, I still got into trouble. This was a strong enough experience that I fully believe I could have constructed a life narrative based on the premise that "you can't win for losing" by carefully selecting from subsequent events in my life.

A few years later, I had an experience that could have shaped a different life narrative. My piano lessons always ended with my piano teacher playing the piece she wanted me to prepare for the next lesson. The problem came when I showed up for my next lesson and played the composition perfectly — in the wrong key. I hadn't studied the music: I'd simply replicated the music I remembered the teacher playing. This showed some musical talent and creativity, but not much discipline. I overheard my mother and the music teacher discussing the event. My mother concluded, "James can accomplish anything he sets his mind to."

These two themes — "You can't win for losing," and "You can accomplish anything you set your mind to" — have shown up throughout my life. Fortunately, accomplishing things has predominated. But the feeling that you can't win for losing seems to be a familiar subtheme.

These competing life narratives were based on events that were emotionally significant but not traumatic. For someone who experiences a major trauma, it is hard not to let that experience dominate the life narrative.

When Gwen tells her life story, it usually begins by her explaining that as a little girl she was sexually abused by her father. She has few childhood memories before that experience, except that she knows she was always considered a very beautiful child. She worries that this is what caused her father to abuse her. As a result she has very ambivalent feelings about being seen as beautiful, even as an adult. One of her deepest fears is that she was somehow responsible for the abuse.

Gwen has always attracted men, but she has always had trouble letting anyone be close. Over the years she has made a number of efforts to establish close relationships, but they were ultimately unsuccessful. The truth is that since the abuse she has been suspicious of all men.

When she met Tony, she was attracted to him because he was warm and emotional. At the same time, she saw in him an opportunity to escape from an impossible family situation. She also felt, at some level, that it was okay to use him, just as she had been used by a man.

For his part, Tony was surprised that she paid any attention to him. In his large and close-knit family, his marriage was seen as proof that Tony was the member of the family to look out for. He was going places.

Tony was always very protective of Gwen and referred to her as his princess. Gwen liked the fact that Tony felt that she was the most beautiful girl he'd ever met. But it also made her feel that she was valued for her beauty, not for who she was as a person. Gwen found that Tony's needs for emotional intimacy made her feel inadequate: they seemed to point out that something was lacking in her. She also experienced his affection more as a demand than as an expression of love.

When they had children, Tony found the emotional warmth he had been lacking with Gwen. Although there was never any spoken agreement on the matter, Gwen handed the primary parenting role over to Tony. If the children had problems, or there were disciplinary issues, Tony handled them. Gwen supervised meals and took care of the house, but she had little real emotional involvement with the children or with her husband.

Gwen was aware that over time the family had created a myth around this dynamic. Everybody agreed that Gwen was highly strung and sensitive and needed to be protected from noise, problems, and emotional outbursts. She did nothing to dispel this notion. Gradually it merged with her "princess" image, and everybody began to think of her as somehow too refined to be involved with everyday issues. The older children learned to protect Gwen from emotional issues and would admonish the younger children not to bother their mother with problems that should be taken to Daddy. When Gwen developed a number of physical ailments that doctors suggested might have an emotional origin, they reinforced her image of being too fragile to deal with the hurly-burly of family life.

When the last child went off to college, Gwen at first felt greatly relieved. Tony found this very upsetting. A few months later, Tony and Gwen's relationship began to seem very much out of balance. Tony kept trying to get Gwen involved in social activities, but she used her physical ailments to beg off. Both felt very lost. Tony tried to cover up his sense of loss with increased activity, while Gwen just became more and more emotionally distant. Tony finally said that Gwen should seek professional help, or else he wanted a divorce.

Childhood sexual abuse is a very painful experience, particularly when the abuser is a parent or trusted adult (such as a coach, teacher, or grandparent). Unfortunately, Gwen had no help in dealing with the situation, and she came to base her life story on the trauma of that experience. The abuse led to a mistrust of men. She both hated and loved being admired for her physical beauty. She felt unable to respond to Tony's demands for emotional intimacy. She essentially signed over all emotional connection with the children to Tony. But when the last child left for college, the

. fundamental lack of intimacy in her life threatened to swamp the relationship. When Gwen started therapy, she felt herself to be a total failure. She had numerous stories of how she had rejected people who had reached out to her, because she felt she was incapable of responding.

Because the abuse was such a central hurt, dealing with it had to be her first goal in therapy. It was clear whenever she recounted these painful experiences that at some level she held herself responsible for them. If she hadn't somehow been attractive to her father, the abuse wouldn't have happened (it hadn't happened with her younger sister). This belief created her ambivalence about being attractive. People who responded to her attractiveness couldn't be trusted, because that had led to the most fundamental violation of trust. Only Tony had been allowed past the initial barriers, but she still withheld genuine closeness even from him.

Gwen decided to go ahead with therapy. Just describing her experience of abuse began to reduce some of its hold over her. Then she was asked to remember experiences where she had been successful in relationships, even if only for a while. Finally, she was asked to remember instances when she had handled challenges without using her beauty, her emotional fragility, or her delicate health. These recollections showed her that even though she had experienced abuse, and that reality would never go away, she could begin to alter some of the emotional edifice she had built on the foundation of that experience.

Over time Gwen began to tell a more balanced life story. It still included the abuse, but that was no longer the story's defining moment. She could remember moments when she'd been fully capable of dealing with life's emotional challenges. She remembered more moments when she felt healthy and well. Slowly she began to feel like a successful, full person, not just a beautiful facade.

Many factors affect recovery from abuse: the type, severity, and duration of the abuse; the age of the child at the time of the abuse; whether any other person or family member knew what happened and believed and supported the child; and the child's own ability to cope with difficult situations. Usually recovery, and the ability to change one's life story, requires the help of a mental health professional trained in this issue.

Family Myths

Individual stories are often reinforced by family myths, which may provide a "necessary fiction" covering up something in the family. Perhaps Daddy abuses alcohol, or Mother is emotionally unstable. Gwen's family created a myth of emotional and physical frailty that explained and accommodated her inability to be emotionally close, permitting the family to act as if things were quite normal.

The problem is that these fictions often become self-fulfilling prophecies. Gwen became a very tense, fragile person and even developed physical ailments consistent with that myth. When the children left home, the accommodation that had permitted Tony and Gwen's relationship to survive was called into question. Gwen needed professional help to heal the wound she experienced in childhood. Tony, too, needed help to see beyond the veneer of the beautiful woman who had provided him with so much status when he married her.

The myth that they created in their marriage could not save their relationship. They had to change the way they related to themselves and each other if they were to survive as a couple.

Family Myths and Life Stories

Typically, the narrative life story must fit within the prevailing family story.

Frank and Edith were raised in families that shared a number of beliefs about marital roles. The husband was seen as the bread-winner and was also responsible for traditionally masculine chores such as cutting the grass, fixing the car, and making sure all the mechanical things around the house were working right. He was also the head of the household, with the final say on all family de-cisions. Both Frank and Edith believed that a good wife should try to please her husband, should not challenge or threaten him, and should take care of all household chores, including child-rearing.

In order to support the family, Frank took a job in Saudi Ara-bia, which paid exceptionally well. He decided it would be best for Edith and the children if they stayed at home. Although Frank sent money home, Edith found herself burdened by her increased responsibilities. She had to make virtually all the decisions about money and take care of household maintenance. With the kids at school, she decided she would like to work, so she took a job managing a small volunteer organization.

When Frank returned home after two years, he and Edith began to argue almost immediately. When he acted in ways he thought a proper husband and father should act, Edith demanded why he thought he was so high-and-mighty. She pointed out that she'd been able to handle things just fine while he was gone. Frank felt he was being rejected, while Edith felt that he was just sweep-ing in after two years away and trying to reduce her to the role of a servant.

Even the simplest things turned into conflicts. When Edith fixed a leaky faucet without first asking Frank to do it, he felt useless and unneeded. Edith viewed Frank's efforts to get her to quit her job as an effort to make her dependent.

Feeling rejected, Frank turned to his parents for moral support. Frank's mother and older sister started to pay Edith visits, pointing out that Edith's behavior was making Frank feel bad. They admonished her to remember that it was a wife's role to be supportive of her husband. Edith's own mother expressed concern about what was happening but admitted for the first time that there had been a time earlier in her own marriage where she had considered getting a divorce.

While Edith got little support from either family, she did receive support from a women's group, where other women talked about similar problems they were having. Several women in the group had decided that the only solution was divorce, having become convinced that "men are just like that," and the only solution was to get along without them. This made Edith feel uncomfortable.

Family myths are finally just that, myths. They help us organize our lives and assign meaning to our experiences, but sometimes they no longer prove useful. When they fail us, we can turn from the old myths and seek new beliefs that can help us make more sense of our lives.

Often, we reject old myths when we begin to feel they are holding us back from realizing our potential. A creative person who thought himself dull may blossom when he breaks free of the family's definition of who he is supposed to be. A woman who has dutifully played the role of good mother may suddenly bloom when she is free of parenting responsibilities — or, like Edith when circumstances required her to essentially be a single parent, she may find herself able to rise to the occasion and display strengths she didn't even know she had. Edith found herself to be a much stronger person than the submissive wife prescribed by her family myth.

In many ways, Frank's case is a tragic one. He does everything according to the rules he was taught. He even follows the rules that Edith and he agreed on when they were first married. But rather than winning him love and respect, his behavior only creates resentment and anger. He's trapped in his own myth, and he doesn't seem to know how to step outside it.

The enforcers come out when the family myth is challenged. Edith has to stand up to a barrage of criticism from family members when she makes her stand. Even her mother is obliged to join the enforcers, but she covertly undermines the effort by acknowledging her own unhappiness in her constrained role.

As the family supports are removed, Edith seeks a new family — in the form of the women's group — to provide her with new beliefs to replace the old. However, she quickly learns that the price of belonging to this surrogate family is to take on a new set of beliefs that might bring her into even greater conflict with family myths — both her own and her husband's.

Changing Your Life Story

It's quite possible that you need to change your life story. Most people don't have the time or commitment to try to change the entire story, so you may want to focus on aspects of your story and your family myths that are the basis for conflict with your partner. If the conflict has to do with child-rearing, sex, or the handling of money, work on those issues.

Here is an activity that you can both engage in that will help you focus on issues of concern:

1. Think of incidents in your past that had something to do with the issues that are causing conflict now. It may help

to break up your life into chapters based on age, or on important events such as a parental divorce or moving to a different city. Childhood experiences are particularly important because you may have developed beliefs based on these experiences without the benefit of understanding the situation from an adult perspective. The purpose of this step is to focus on those issues you want to address.

2. Now look for incidents where you, or someone you admire, acted differently than you believe you and your partner should act now. How did those incidents turn out? Did they have the outcome you would have predicted, or did something different happen? How do you feel about the "characters" in these dramas?

I think you'll be surprised how many such incidents you'll remember. Don't expect them all to emerge immediately. It may take several days for them to pop into consciousness.

You may discover a wider range of past behaviors than you thought possible. Some of the incidents you recall may confirm your present feelings, but you may also recall experiences that show other possible behaviors and possible outcomes.

One of the ways to reframe your life is to change your self-talk. We program and reprogram ourselves with the inner voice that offers a running commentary on our behaviors and life events. Developing positive self-talk, as discussed in the next chapter, is an effective way of reframing ourselves.

Summary

When you tell your life story, you make choices about what events and incidents are included. These choices create the frame through which you view your life. One way to change your life is to change the story you tell yourself about it. In the process you may rediscover neglected parts of your life story that can lead you to emphasize different capabilities and see yourself in a different light.

Individual stories are often reinforced by family myths. These myths help us organize our lives and assign meaning to our experiences, but when they no longer prove useful, we can seek new beliefs that can better help us make sense of our lives.

CHAPTER THIRTEEN

Self-Talk

Examine your self-talk to be sure it is serving you well,
and reprogram it when you need to.

If you've ever made a bad mistake, you may have heard an inner voice saying, "That was sure a dumb thing to do." We all have an inner voice that comments on what we are doing, for better or for worse.

Don't think you have an inner voice? Pay attention to your thoughts when you are:

- trying to remember what you need at the store.
- working to stay calm when you are upset.
- practicing asking for a raise.
- telling yourself to stop eating.
- getting yourself to do one more lap.
- thinking of a witty retort after the fact.

You will probably notice that your inner voice is present and helping you get ready or make sense of what has happened.

Psychologists refer to this inner dialogue as *self-talk*. Everybody does it.

Why does this matter for handling conflict between couples? Changing your self-talk is a powerful way of changing your beliefs about yourself. You and your spouse can each work on changing attitudes and behaviors that lead to conflicts by changing your self-talk.

Self-talk is like computer software. It tells us what to do and how to feel about events and situations. A lot of self-talk feeds us valuable information that serves us well, that helps us succeed and even ensures our survival. For example, "Look both ways before crossing the street" and "Stand up for yourself" are constructive reminders.

But other self-talk undermines us and keeps us from experiencing parts of our personality. Your inner voice may be telling you things like this:

- I just know it won't work.
- It's just no use.
- I'm just not creative.
- I never have enough time.
- I never know what to say.
- I'm just not academically inclined.
- Things just aren't working out right for me.
- I don't have the energy I used to have.
- I'm just not good at math.
- I wish I could sing, but I just don't have a good voice.
- I'm terrified of public speaking.
- I'm just not musical.
- I'm really at the end of my rope.
- Everything I touch turns to [*bleep*].

When you read this list, you may even hear it in the voice of the person who first said these things to you. Your father may have told you that you were lousy at math. You may have overheard your mother tell your grandmother that you just weren't academically inclined, and then heard her say the same thing to you.

I wince whenever I hear an adult tell a child something like "You're stupid" or "Academics are just not your strength." If you want a person to act stupidly, both as a child and as an adult, telling them they're stupid is a reliable way to program them.

Most of our self-talk consists of beliefs programmed into us when we were children. We heard these beliefs so often, or in such emotionally intense situations, that now we believe them and repeat them to ourselves whenever the occasion arises. But do you really want major decisions about your life made by a four-year-old or an eight-year-old? That's what's happening when we accept negative self-talk as the truth about us and about life. Some of our basic attitudes toward ourselves are rooted in unexamined childhood programming.

Start paying attention to your self-talk. Write down some of the attitudes expressed during self-talk. Ask yourself, would I say to a friend the things I say to myself? Probably not. As adults, we know that saying negative things is hurtful and destroys friendships. So why do we say such things to ourselves? As a general rule, don't say anything to yourself that you wouldn't say to other people.

Working on your self-talk is a good way to challenge the idea that there's some inherent flaw in your personality. If you have deficits, you are not doomed to live with them forever; you can change your programming. When that changes, you may find you have hidden strengths where previously you had problems.

Sometimes self-talk imparts conventional wisdom that is at

odds with changes we're trying to bring about in ourselves or with others. For example, here are some self-talk phrases about conflict that many people would accept without thought:

- Whenever anybody says anything bad about me, I must correct them by pointing out their personal flaws.
- The best defense is a good offense.
- There are winners and losers — and I'm going to be a winner.
- People who disagree with me are opponents to be overcome.
- Once I've picked the best option, I need to hang on to it and defend it.

These phrases all describe a win/lose model of conflict resolution, and they all make it harder to reach a mutually acceptable solution to conflict. If you approach conflict with these attitudes, your relationship will be the loser.

Moving to Positive Self-Talk

So how do we change negative self-talk? Using the computer programming analogy, we need to overwrite the negative programs and replace them with a new program. It sounds easy, but it is hard work.

Here are the basic steps in reprogramming your negative self-talk to positive self-talk:

Watch for the Self-Talk Statements about Yourself

The first step is to pay attention to your self-talk and identify any that is negative. You won't be able to change your negative self-talk without noticing it and making a conscious choice to change it.

Some people find it helpful to keep a self-talk log. Carry a small notebook, and every time you notice a negative self-talk thought, write it in the log.

Monitor the Self-Talk of People around You

Sometimes it is easier to see the impact of negative self-talk by noticing its effect on other people. Obviously, you won't be able to listen in on their inner self-talk, but people often speak their self-talk out loud: "I'm just not good at those sorts of things," "I haven't got time to deal with that," "I've always wanted to do that, but I just don't have what it takes." How does their self-talk limit them? Do they stop doing things they should or want to do? Do they avoid new behaviors that might be helpful or just plain fun?

Identify Negative Self-Talk That You Want to Change

Next, identify those areas you want to work on. A lot of self-talk is useful. What kinds of self-talk are giving you a problem?

Since we're working on conflict resolution between loved ones, here are some of the issues and skills you might be thinking about:

- accepting that the other person has a different emotional reality
- listening until you understand the other person — and they feel understood
- learning to express feelings rather than judgments
- avoiding seeing the other person as an adversary
- learning not to personalize everything that is said about a situation — being less defensive
- believing that there are many possible solutions, not just the one you thought of

If you have negative self-talk that makes it hard to make these changes, those phrases might be a place to start your work to re-duce negative self-talk.

Eliminate Internal Negative Chatter ("Cancel, Cancel")

Once you've learned to notice your negative self-talk, you can work on actively resisting it when it occurs.

Here are a couple of things that can help eliminate negative self-talk:

- Some people wear a rubber band and snap themselves with it whenever they start to engage in negative self-talk. (I've never tried this, but I'm told it works.)
- Some people set up an internal signal, such as telling themselves, "Cancel, cancel," that tells them to stop the negative self-talk.

Replace Negative Self-Talk with Positive Self-Talk

You are always going to engage in self-talk, but it doesn't have to be negative. The trick is to use it to help you. Change your self-talk so that you program yourself with the behaviors and at-titudes that help.

Look for phrases that really resonate with you, things you re-ally feel. Here are some phrases that a friend uses:

- I love you, and I'm feeling very [emotion] right now and need some time out.
- I can calm down and finish this conversation.
- I know I am okay and can handle this.
- I trust that [person] loves me.

- We have worked things out before and will again this time.
- I can control myself and my behavior.
- I trust myself to speak up for myself.
- I can take care of myself no matter what.
- It is okay for me to let go and trust right now.
- I have everything I need to be able to do this.
- I can stay right here and remain calm and confident.
- What is happening right now is not about me.
- I choose not to react and be pulled into what is going on.
- I trust I can talk to my partner about this later.
- I can manage myself.
- I can ask for help.
- I am not alone.
- I can lean on other people.
- I can lean on my partner.
- It is okay for me to have whatever feelings I have.
- I can choose how I act.
- If I trust myself I can act differently.
- I am a good listener. I am attentive, interested, and aware of everything that is going on around me.
- I have the courage to share my feelings. I take responsibility for everything I say and do.

Some phrases may hit you as icky-sweet, while others give you a feeling of hope and real promise. Just ignore the icky-sweet ones and pay attention to the ones that give you a charge of energy.

You need to find your own phrases to address the issues you are working on. You need the emotional investment that comes from choosing phrases that have meaning for you. Write your positive self-help phrases in the present tense, as if the desired change has already taken place.

Below are examples of ways to replace negative self-talk phrases with positive ones:

Negative self-talk	Positive self-talk
I've never done it before.	I'm doing it, and I like it.
It's too complicated.	I'm figuring it out one step at a time until I understand the whole thing.
I don't have the resources.	I'm starting with what I've got, and trusting that small successes will attract resources.
It's too big a change.	I've assessed the risks, and I believe the possible benefits are well worth the risks.
No one bothers to communicate with me.	I am reaching out to other people, and will attract relationships with the people I need.
I'm not going to get any better at this.	I'm continuing to do this, knowing I'm getting better with practice.

You probably didn't like some of these phrases. Maybe they sounded too Pollyannaish, or you wanted something stronger — or less strong. Write your own phrases in the spaces on the next page or in a notebook.

Negative self-talk	Positive self-talk
I've never done it before.	
It's too complicated.	
I don't have the resources.	
It's too big a change.	
No one bothers to communicate with me.	
I'm not going to get any better at this.	

Now try identifying the issues you want to work on, then write down the positive self-help phrases that will help you with these issues.

Negative self-talk	Positive self-talk

The essential ingredient in any effort to change negative self-talk is repetition. You've been repeating the old self-talk for years, and it will take a while to overwrite this programming. Some people have even reported that it seemed like the old programming tried to talk them out of the new programming. It's important to select positive self-talk phrases that have meaning and power for you, phrases that you like hearing. Persist!

Here are some of the techniques people use to program positive self-talk phrases:

Mirror, mirror on the wall: First thing in the morning, as you are in the bathroom preparing for your day, repeat your positive self-talk phrases aloud to your image in the mirror. Do this a minimum of ten times. Say the phrases with energy and enthusiasm.

Sticky notes: One way to remind yourself of your new positive programming is to put sticky notes up in visible places. The note doesn't have to contain the whole phrase, just enough of a cue to trigger the full phrase in your mind.

3X5″ cards: Some people put their positive self-talk phrases on 3×5″ index cards. During the day they take out the cards and read the phrases aloud.

Tape talk: One of the most effective ways to reprogram your self-talk is to play audio recordings of the new phrases. There are professional recordings available, but if you want to use your own personal phrases, you can make your own. Most smartphones can record and play your phrases. People in the field of psychology claim that playing these recordings quietly in the background while doing something else is a particularly effective approach.

Surround Yourself with Positive People

Some friends will try to make you stay the same person you've always been. Whether they're comfortable with the old self or threatened by the new self, they will reinforce your old programs.

Even if they don't criticize your new behavior, they may be so full of negative self-talk themselves that being around them undermines your efforts to change. Notice what it feels like to be around people who have positive programming and who encourage your new positive attitudes and behaviors.

Many of us discover not only that we need to reprogram our self-talk, but that different parts of our personality say different things. The next chapter looks at ways to get to know those parts of us and discover who's in charge.

Summary

We all have an inner voice that comments on what we are doing, for better or for worse. Psychologists refer to this inner dialogue as *self-talk*. You and your partner can work on changing attitudes and behaviors that lead to conflicts by each working with your self-talk. Negative self-talk is very common; it traps us into attitudes we learned as children and have not subjected to conscious reexamination. You are always going to engage in self-talk, but you can learn to notice it and reprogram it so that it is not negative but rather supportive of the changes you're trying to make.

CHAPTER FOURTEEN

Who Speaks for Your Internal Committee?

Get to know the different parts of your personality
and get them talking to each other.

Whenever Randy and Julia get into conflicts that involve different emotional realities, it is almost as if their personalities change. Randy becomes very judgmental. Even though he thinks of himself as a fairly open-minded person, he suddenly becomes very dogmatic. His beliefs are absolutes. Julia, on the other hand, seems to become very rebellious, much like an upset eight-year-old child, driving Randy crazy. It almost seems as if they become different people.

In one sense, that's true. In each of them, different subpersonalities come to the fore; or, as some psychologists describe it, they are now in different *ego states*. Most of us think of ourselves as a single, unitary personality. Yet we often experience divisions that make us feel torn, as if there are separate and distinct personalities warring within us. We even describe it that way: "One part of me says I should go ahead and do it, but another part of me cautions me against it."

Some years ago I had lunch with a psychotherapist I know. After I'd shared some feelings about a situation, his question was "Which member of the committee feels that way?" His penetrating question raises a fundamental and important question for couples wrestling with differing emotional realities. Conflicts rooted in different perceptions of reality may trigger parts of your personality — different members of your internal "committee" — that dominate during the argument and even take fixed positions that make other parts of the personality uncomfortable.

When Randy and Julia switch into their dogmatic and childish roles, they are locked in what some psychologists would call a parent-child relationship. The parent and child parts of ourselves are particularly likely to be triggered as conflicts escalate, and they contribute to further escalation of the conflict. The parent self in Randy confronts Julia with criticisms or threats. Julia reacts as the child, fighting for her individuality against the overbearing parent who, years before, humiliated her. The inner child, threatened by a potential loss of love, slips into emotions and behaviors associated with earlier times.

When a conflict occurs, any one of several different selves might take the lead. We may respond with a relatively realistic or objective appraisal of conditions, but, equally likely, we may respond from the perspective of the child who believes that what they experience is absolute truth.

Resolving disputes over differing emotional realities requires soul-searching to understand who is speaking for our personal committee, and why.

Modern consciousness researchers tell us that the human personality is composed of different ego states, parts, or selves. Ego states are sets of feelings, accompanied by related sets of behavior patterns. Other therapists go further, describing these parts of the personality as "distinct personalities, each with a full range of emotion and desire, and of different ages, temperaments, talents, and even genders." Psychologists' understanding of these subpersonalities has evolved over time.

Sigmund Freud saw the psyche as consisting of three parts: the id, ego, and superego. The id is the impulsive (and unconscious) part of our psyche that contains sexual and aggressive drives and hidden memories — all of our most basic animal and primitive impulses. According to Freud, we are born with the id intact. The ego develops early in childhood to mediate between the unrealistic id and the external real world. It is the decision-making component of personality, mediating between the desires of the id and the moral constraints of the superego. The superego is like a conscience, reflecting social standards learned from adults important to us during childhood.

Freud's theory is just that, a theory. Except in psychoanalytic circles, Freud's theory is no longer considered central to psychology. However, Freudian thinking underlies much subsequent psychological thought. Among the most influential ideas are the following:

- The psyche is made up of parts or subpersonalities that compete or attempt to control each other.
- These parts are shaped by childhood experiences.
- Our behavior is controlled by conceptions of our ideal self and by constraints we learn in childhood (and thereafter).
- Portions of our psyche are unconscious mental processes, accessible through indirect means such as dreams, hypnosis, mental imagery, and "Freudian slips."

Transactional Analysis

Probably the best-known theory about the composition of the psyche is *transactional analysis*, which was very popular in the 1960s and 1970s. Transactional analysis was a theory (and a movement) based on the work of Dr. Eric Berne, who trained in Freudian psychoanalysis and practiced as a psychotherapist for many years. He was the author of the bestselling books *Games People Play* and *What Do You Say After You Say Hello?* Other authors popularized transactional analysis concepts in books such as *I'm OK, You're OK* (Thomas A. Harris) and *Scripts People Live* (Claude Steiner). Transactional analysis concepts were so popular that they showed up in songs, movies, and cartoons.

The core concept of transactional analysis is that there are three ego states: the parent, the adult, and the child (see diagram). Berne defined an ego state as "a consistent pattern of feeling and experience directly related to a corresponding consistent pattern of behavior." Our different ego states invite different responses from those we interact with. Our behaviors associated with the parent ego state evoke entirely different reactions from those of the adult or child ego state. The other person's response, in turn, evokes different behaviors from us, depending on both their ego state and our own. At their simplest, the three ego states are as follows:

Parent Ego State

Behaviors, thoughts, and feelings copied from parents or parent figures

Adult Ego State

Behaviors, thoughts, and feelings that are direct responses to the here and now

Child Ego State

Behaviors, thoughts, and feelings replayed from childhood

Parent: A state in which people behave, feel, and think in unconscious mimicry of the actions of their parents (or other parental figures), or of the way they interpreted their parents' actions. If parents or other important adults were demanding, judgmental, or aggressive, the child internalizes those behaviors. If parents were loving, supportive, and caring, those behaviors become part of the adult ego state. The parent internalizes admonitions such as the following:

- Never talk to strangers.
- Always chew with your mouth closed.
- Look both ways before you cross the street.

Adult: This ego state engages in an objective appraisal of reality. It processes information and makes predictions about major emotions that could affect its operation. Harris describes the adult as "a data-processing computer, which grinds out decisions after computing the information from three sources: the Parent, the Child, and the data which the Adult has gathered and is gathering."

Child: A state in which people behave, feel, and think similarly to the ways they did in childhood. The child is the source of emotions, creation, recreation, spontaneity, and intimacy. The child retains the emotions or feelings associated with external events. Berne believed the child ego state is substantially formed by the age of five.

It's easy to draw parallels between Berne's three ego states and Freud's id, ego, and superego. But Berne was very emphatic that the ego states he was describing were fundamentally different from Freud's scheme. The id, ego, and superego, Berne argued, were just concepts. Ego states, he believed, could be actually observed through people's behavior, both in his individual patients and in all social transactions.

Over time, Berne postulated that both the parent and child ego states had positive and negative sides. In fact, these different sides were essentially separate ego states. There was a nurturing parent (NP), conveying acceptance, nurturing, and caring. There was a controlling parent, who was primarily involved in promoting rules, shoulds, and musts. There was a free child, full of energy and fun; and there was an adapted child, who was rebellious and eager to undermine authority.

Berne argued that when ego states interacted, they produced a "transaction" that might be either productive or negative (hence the name *transactional analysis*). One of the key goals of his approach was to identify the ego states involved and why they produced the positive or negative results.

The simplest form of transaction is between two people in adult ego states. For example, one person might ask, "Have you seen my watch? I must have put it down somewhere." The other person might respond with: "Yes, I think I saw it on the kitchen counter." Both people are satisfied with the exchange.

But it doesn't always go like that, as any married couple can tell you. It could go like this:

> "Have you seen my watch? I must have put it down some-
> where."
> "Why can't you keep track of your own things? I'm tired
> of picking up after you."

Or it might go like this:

> "Have you seen my watch? I must have put it down some-
> where."
> "You always blame me for everything."

In both cases the initial request is a simple adult request for information (though a different intent might be conveyed by tone of voice). In the first example, the second person responds from the controlling parent ego state. In the second example, the response comes from the adapted child. Neither response produces a satisfactory transaction.

Transactional analysis therapy seeks to help individuals identify the behaviors associated with each of their ego states. The behaviors associated with one person's parent state may be significantly different from those of another person's parent state. Because the parent is an internalized version of the individual's real parents (and/or other significant adults), each individual has a unique parent ego state. (The parent ego state does not necessarily represent how the parent actually acted but rather how the parent was perceived by the child.)

When analyzing transactions, we must look beyond *what* is being said to *how* it is being said: emphasis on particular words, changes in tone, volume, and so on. Nonverbal signs, such as body language and facial expressions, are also part of the transaction. Research by Dr. Albert Mehrabian shows that the listener focuses on three sources of information in the following proportions:

- Actual words: 7 percent
- The way words are delivered (tone, emphasis on certain words, etc.): 38 percent
- Facial expressions: 55 percent

Family Therapy

Traditional therapy took the form of a confidential meeting between a therapist and an individual patient, to ensure that patients were not inhibited in sharing their feelings. But in the 1960s, therapists began working with nuclear and extended families. Family therapy is based on the premise that the family is the source of the dominant forces in our lives and provides the main context in which the individual operates. People are the products of their context: to understand the individual, you need to understand the context. Change the dynamics of the family, and you can change the lives of every member of the family.

Some of the fundamental premises of family therapy are as follows:

- The family is a *system*. A system is more than the sum of its parts: it is an organic whole whose members operate in a way that transcends their individuality. The primary issue is the pattern of the interaction within the system.
- Individuals can get locked into roles by family expectations. Roles tend to be reciprocal and complementary.

A domineering partner, for example, requires a submissive mate. Parents may get locked into complementary roles of strictness and leniency. These roles reinforce each other. Neither person is likely to change unless the other does.

- Problems are sustained by ongoing actions and reactions. Each action by one member of the family influences the actions of the others, in a circular pattern. Soon it is not even clear who started the behavior. Nor does it matter.
- It is essential to examine how people talk with each other — the process, rather than the content.
- Families must undergo change to accommodate the changing maturity and life demands of their members.
- Each family member constructs a life narrative. While this narrative makes sense of their experience, it may also limit the range of "permissible" behavior.
- Family members use only some of the full range of behaviors available to them. Family therapy can help them expand their range of behaviors.

One of the key concepts of family therapy is the concept of *burdens.* If someone experiences a major trauma, they are likely to carry around a burden of emotional pain for many years. Burdens can also come from a family dynamic. You may know couples who achieve a functional balance only because one partner compensates for the other. Charlie spends money too freely; Isabel, his wife, watches every nickel and dime. Both carry a burden. Isabel carries the burden of protecting the family from financial ruin. Charlie carries the burden of compensating for her tight-fistedness.

Families may actually assign burdens to their members. In practical terms, this may mean that one family member must take on supporting the family financially, while another may have to take care of an elderly parent. But it also happens in their emotional life. If the father is a perfectionist, one child may become a perfectionist, while another may rebel against perfectionism. Both are burdened by the father's perfectionism. A child whose parents withhold approval is likely to carry the burden of a search for approval into adult life. Others may carry the burden of having to be a great success, caring for the emotional needs of another family member, or compensating for a family member's behavior (such as alcohol abuse).

Getting Parts of the Psyche to Talk to Each Other

Dr. Richard Schwartz is a leading light in the field known as *internal family systems therapy* (IFS). This approach combines principles of family therapy with the concept that the self is made up of many different parts. We all, according to Schwartz, "contain many different beings." The challenge is learning to get all these parts of the self to talk to one another, to draw on the strengths of each of the parts to meet life's inevitable tests.

Therapists Hal and Sidra Stone, pioneers of the "psychology of selves," put it this way: "Each of us 'contains multitudes.' We are made up of many selves, identifying with some and rejecting others. This over-identification with some selves and the loss of wholeness that comes from the rejection of others can create imbalances and blind spots. This work is about embracing all the selves. This dance of the selves is an amazing process and we see the dynamics of the world around us shift as our internal world changes."

Schwartz and other IFS therapists believe that the techniques of family therapy can be used to conduct this conversation.

"People are viewed as having all the resources they need, rather than as having a disease or deficit. Instead of lacking resources, people are seen as being constrained from using innate strengths by polarized relationships both within themselves and with the people around them."

Parts of the self take on burdens. Other parts protect us from being overwhelmed by our burdens. There are no "bad" parts; rather, parts may become stuck in extreme roles in an attempt to cope with difficult life circumstances and traumatic experiences.

One of the goals of IFS therapy is to help people understand these burdens and release them. It accomplishes this by getting the parts of the personality to talk with each other, identifying burdens that have immobilized or twisted things out of balance.

IFS does not assume that each of us has the same internal cast of characters, such as adult, parent, and child. Instead, each of us may have numerous internal parts, which we name for ourselves. As the psychotherapist Jay Earley puts it: "The human mind isn't a unitary thing that sometimes has irrational feelings. It is a complex system of interacting *parts*, each with a mind of its own. It's like an internal family — with wounded children, impulsive teenagers, rigid adults, hypercritical parents, caring friends, nurturing relatives, and so on."

Earley adds:

Each part has a role to play in your life; it brings a quality to your psyche and your actions in the world. Each tries to advance your interests in some way (even if sometimes it has the opposite effect). Some parts govern the way you handle practical tasks in your life. Some protect against external threats or internal pain. Some are open and friendly with people. Others hold unresolved fear or shame from your childhood. Some are performers;

others solitary thinkers. Some care for people, while others affect the way you feel about yourself. And so on.

Implications for Arguments over Differing Emotional Realities

So why does this matter for couples in conflict over different emotional realities? Simply put, the impasse you are experiencing may have less to do with deep philosophical differences than with certain parts of yourselves that are engaged in a power struggle. As Richard Schwartz puts it: "The critical or hurtful things that loved ones say about us in arguments may not represent their 'real' feelings, but instead may be the opinion of only one or two angry personalities within them, while a silent majority of other personalities may remain loving."

Let's go back to Randy and Julia. Every time they get in an argument, Randy slips into a parental ego state (controlling parent) and Julia slips into a child ego state (adapted child). Most of the time, communication between a controlling parent and a rebellious child sets off an argument no matter what positions they take. So long as each of them is reacting to the other's ego state, it's very hard to judge whether their disagreement is based in deeply held beliefs or dug-in defensiveness. If they were able to communicate adult to adult, we might discover that they are not as far apart as it appears.

Each of you may have a part of your personality that speaks as if it represents the total personality. Other parts of you might feel very differently, but you'll never know it, because the subpersonality that is acting as spokesperson when you get in an argument is expressing only its own views, not those of the entire psyche.

Another possibility is that the conflict is rooted in dynamics within your family systems. Perhaps — for reasons that will require some psychological work to discover — each person is responding to a burden or expectation put on them by their families of origin. When they can put down those burdens, they may find that their differences are not as great as they imagined.

Getting to Know the Members of Your Committee

All three therapeutic approaches discussed here — transactional analysis, family therapy, and internal family systems therapy — evolved in the context of therapist-client relationships. A knowledgeable third party, someone who is not part of the family system, can be invaluable in helping you to understanding family dynamics, both external and internal. If you think the family dynamics we've discussed in this chapter could be clouding your relationships, I encourage you to consider working with a therapist. The appendix includes resources and advice for finding a suitable therapist.

Working with a therapist is too time-consuming and expensive for many people. You can adapt some of the same therapeutic approaches to use on your own and with your partner. You may want to do more reading about the particular approach you want to take.

If you want to establish communication with the various parts of your personality, whether the parent, adult, and child of transactional analysis or the personalized parts discussed in IFS, you first need to recognize the parts. Psychotherapists agree that there are certain ways of talking, identifiable attitudes, and even individualized body sensations associated with each part. It's a bit like meeting someone you know but have never explicitly recognized as a distinct entity.

Here are some techniques you can employ without a therapist to get in touch with the different parts of your personality.

Journaling: Keep a running journal of what's going on in you during the day. Note in particular whether different characters seem to be appearing in your psychological life. Ask those characters to tell you more about themselves. Record what thoughts occur to you without a lot of screening or judgments. If you can, establish a kind of written conversation with these parts of self. It doesn't matter if it's all imaginary — you'll still be learning about your inner life.

Mental imagery: If you are good at seeing mental images, you may find mental imagery a useful approach. Here's a place to start:

- Do some relaxation exercises, or something that helps you get very relaxed (no alcohol, please).
- Close your eyes.
- In your mind's eye, see yourself someplace where you are safe and secure.
- In the distance, see someone coming toward you.
- As this person comes closer, it seems to be someone you know well, someone very wise.
- Ask this person who they are, and ask them what they know about the various parts of your psyche.
- You may even ask this person to introduce you to some of your other parts.
- Allow these parts to join you, and have a conversation about what role they play in your psyche.
- Some questions to ask include:
    - the name of the part
    - what it feels emotionally
    - what it looks like
    - where it's located in your body, and what it feels like

- what its job is
- how it makes you behave
- what it wants
- When you are ready to stop, thank your guest(s) for helping you, and say goodbye.
- See yourself in your safe place once again.
- Open your eyes.

Empty chair: Sit facing an empty chair. Imagine that the chair is occupied by someone else, or a part of yourself. Say what you need to say to that person or part. Listen for any response from the imagined person or part. If there is, have a conversation. You may want to ask some of the questions listed in the mental imagery exercise above.

The point is to try to establish communications with your inner parts. Once you've established a link, you may want to discuss what role your various parts play in the conflict with your partner. In particular, find out whether all the parts are in agreement, or whether some parts are misrepresenting themselves as speaking for your entire psyche.

Our internal differences raise issues that need to be addressed, and these encounters with the various parts of our personality can be a source of much learning.

Summary

Modern consciousness researchers tell us that the human personality is composed of different ego states, parts, or selves, which interact in different ways with the world and people around us. Various schools of psychotherapy have described these parts in different ways. The conflicts between a couple may have less to do with deep philosophical differences than with particular parts of yourselves being engaged in a power struggle. Each of you may have a part of the personality that is speaking as if it represents the total personality, drowning out other parts of you that might feel very differently. A trained therapist, or exercises you undertake on your own, can help you identify the parts of yourself that may be involved in these conflicts and establish communication with them.

CHAPTER FIFTEEN

The Value of Being Different

Accept that differences can make
your relationships richer.

People often feel threatened by the fact that their loved ones have separate realities. They may fear that to be different is to be separate; that if a couple has differences, the relationship is in trouble; that differences mean their partner does not love them; or that if there are differences, they'll have to give up their own sense of self to be in a relationship with the other person.

These are fears, not facts. Actually, the stronger the relationship, the more differences you can handle. Think of any argument that you've ever had that was actually fun. It was probably with an old and dear friend. You knew that no matter what position either of you took, you'd still be friends afterward. When a relationship is solid, your argument is about a specific subject, not whether the relationship will continue. When the relationship is insecure, everything you say could jeopardize it. You can see this when you are just getting to know people. What you say could determine whether you will be friends, so you are cautious about expressing your views.

All couples have disagreements. The issue is how you handle them. Dr. John Gottman, who has conducted extensive research on couples and conflict, has concluded that the most important characteristic of a successful relationship is how couples handle the healing after an argument.

It is true that when you normally feel very close, disagreement can create a feeling of separateness. What's critical is whether you feel that you are both working together to resolve the differences. If you are taking rigid positions — my side, your side — then the sense of separateness will grow stronger.

The idea that if people disagree with you they don't love you is a child's view of reality. Your adult self knows better. No relationship would survive if that were the test. If you believe that disagreement signals a lack of love you are setting up a situation where the other person feels that to be in relationship with you, they must give up themselves. If the price of staying in a relationship is that one person has to give up their sense of self, then you and your partner need some professional help.

Travelers in foreign countries often find that through observing other cultures, they learn a great deal about their own culture. The same is true of cultures within families. Family myths and culture are like a glass dome. When you are inside the dome, you don't know you are enclosed: you are usually so deeply immersed in your family culture that you are scarcely aware of the way it shapes your life. As the psychologist James C. Coleman has remarked, "The fish will be the last to discover water." People who know no other cultural patterns but their own tend to regard them as God-given and intrinsically right.

Just as we discover our own cultures by getting to know other cultures, so we learn more about our own emotional realities by learning to accept and getting to know the virtues of our partner's emotional realities.

You learn to manage your differences by sharing them, not by hiding them. If both people in a relationship are willing to do this, you can create a shared reality that fits you both, freeing you both to enjoy each other's uniqueness. Though it may seem like a contradiction, the quality of our relationships improves in direct proportion to our willingness to acknowledge our differences.

This is the basis for another of the guidelines. Live with the disagreement: engage it emotionally, don't gloss it over and pretend it has gone away.

Kali and Elizabeth have been married for seven years, but lately they've been having disagreements about how to raise their children. Kali was raised in a traditional Hawaiian family. There was a lot of love, but there were also frequent cuffs, swats, and spankings. Elizabeth was raised in a family where there was no corporal punishment, but there was lots of shaming and guilt. Elizabeth vowed that she would never subject her children to the guilt trips that she felt her parents laid on her.

Kali describes his parenting style as "strict." Elizabeth can't stand it when he spanks the kids. Kali sees her as a weak parent, unable to set or enforce limits. He says he is just raising the kids the way he was raised, and "I turned out okay." But this has the effect of turning any criticisms of his child-rearing approach into a criticism of him personally. Lately child-rearing has become such a big issue that it threatens their relationship. They have decided to use techniques described in this book to try to resolve their differences.

First Kali and Elizabeth tried active listening (chapter 7), but they found that they couldn't really stay with it. After one or two active-listening responses, they would start arguing. Instead they tried the Five-Minute Rule (also discussed in chapter 7). This worked better because there was an absolute ban on interruptions while the other person was speaking. They also agreed to use "I" messages (chapter 6), avoiding blame and accusation. This prevented arguments from escalating, but both Kali and Elizabeth admitted that they slipped back into sending "you" messages occasionally.

Next, they tried out collaborative problem-solving (chapter 9). One of the major results from this process was an agreement that they would attend a parenting class together. Neither of them had received any training in parenting. From the class, they learned that most people, unless they've received some training, act much as they perceived their own parents did (which may not be an accurate representation of the way the parents actually acted). They also learned some new techniques for managing their kids' behavior, such as using time-outs. But the biggest benefit came from being able to talk openly about these issues with other parents.

As an assignment for the class, Kali and Elizabeth examined their personal values (see chapter 10) and constructed a values continuum for their child-rearing goals. The idea is to show a positive good at each end of the continuum, then have each person indicate where they would put the balance point between the two goods. Kali and Elizabeth's continuum ended up looking like the diagram below.

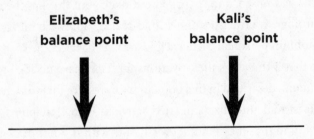

Elizabeth's balance point   **Kali's balance point**

Spontaneity, creativity   Self-discipline, responsibility

Elizabeth places somewhat greater emphasis on spontaneity and creativity for her children. Kali is more concerned that the children learn self-discipline and responsibility. But although this continuum reflects their differences in philosophy, the big thing that Kali and Elizabeth noticed was that their views were actually quite close. They leaned toward opposite ends of the continuum, but they were not in fundamental disagreement.

Even so, Kali and Elizabeth decided they needed professional help and agreed to go together to a psychotherapist. The therapist worked with Kali on getting in touch with his inner little boy. To Kali's surprise, he discovered memories of being terrified of the physical punishment his father had used. Rather than remembering it as a positive thing, he now realized that he had lived in fear of his father for most of his childhood. This discovery made him very uncomfortable and challenged some of his beliefs about the value of strict child-rearing.

Elizabeth discovered that setting and maintaining boundaries was an issue in several areas of her life, not just with the children. She was good at getting other people to feel guilty, but not good at setting limits without blame and accusation. She decided she wanted to continue with additional parenting training, to learn techniques for setting and maintaining limits without resorting to corporal punishment or guilt trips.

Elizabeth and Kali are still working on resolving their differences about parenting styles, but they feel like they've made considerable progress. Kali is unlikely to resort to physical punishment except in very unusual circumstances. Elizabeth is getting training on setting limits without guilt trips. But probably the biggest payoff is their feeling of working together to address the issues and the enhancement of their overall relationship.

Kali and Elizabeth have been willing to spend considerable

time and emotional effort to resolve their differences. This shows great commitment to the relationship.

Summary

How couples (or friends) deal with differences depends on the strength of the relationship. When a relationship is solid, differences on specific issues do not threaten it; when the relationship is insecure, however, any point of disagreement can jeopardize it. The stronger the relationship, the more differences you can handle. You learn to manage your differences by sharing them, not by hiding them. If you can do this, you begin creating a shared reality that fits you both and allows each of you to appreciate one another's uniqueness. Though it may seem like a contradiction, the quality of our relationships improves in direct proportion to our willingness to acknowledge our differences. Examining those differences may actually reveal that the distance between our points of view is not as great as we originally believed.

Conclusion

How do you resolve disputes based on different emotional realities? Here are some of the guidelines I've recommended.

Agree that each person has a right to his or her way of seeing and experiencing things (his or her emotional reality) while affirming and trusting your own.

This idea is the foundation stone of this book. If you try to insist that other people experience reality the same way you do, you're in trouble. Lots of conflicts will come your way. You've got to accept that everybody has a reality of their own. They don't have the same reactions to things that you do. The sooner you let go of the idea that there is something wrong with them for feeling the way they do, the happier you — and they — will be.

Communicate your own reality without finding fault with other people's.

Most fights begin with blaming and accusing. We need to learn how to tell people what we are feeling without making them responsible for our feelings. "I" messages are an important tool for sharing feelings without blame or accusation. You can't control how the other person reacts, but you can minimize the chances that they will feel and act defensive.

Listen — with both your head and your heart — even though you may continue to disagree.

Listening is a key skill in any kind of conflict resolution, but it must be done with both the head and the heart. Active listening is a way to express this attitude. When you are both upset and can't use active listening, use some technique like the Five-Minute Rule to make sure both people get to express themselves without constant contradiction.

Learn to identify behaviors that cause fights to escalate, and set mutually acceptable rules to limit these behaviors.

Fights don't get out of control all by themselves. It is our own behaviors that make them escalate. Learn to identify behaviors that cause fights to escalate and agree with your partner to stop them. Even if your partner won't agree, stop your own escalating behaviors. It's easy, when someone has a different way of perceiving reality, to see that person as an adversary. Remember to protect your relationship even when you are in conflict. You want there to be some "We" left once the fight is over.

Use a problem-solving process that says "We have a problem," not "You are the problem."

Using a structured problem-solving process like that shown in chapter 9 provides guidance, enabling you to determine where you are on the road toward resolving your differences. This process is based on a good deal of research. Above all, the goal of the problem-solving process is for you to stand side by side, facing out, taking the attitude that *we* have a problem rather than seeing one another as the problem.

Look for the positive good that your partner supports, even when your partner opposes what you think is important.

Values choices inherently require us to decide the relative importance of two different things that are both good. For example, personal freedom and societal well-being are both good, but sometimes to get one you've got to give up some of the other. When we argue, we quickly become polarized, reflexively opposing one another's positions. Look instead for the positive value your partner is seeking. You'll probably find that you support the same value, but you don't think it as important as another value in the present situation. Focusing on the good your partner wants helps keep you from seeing your partner as an adversary.

Seek out new ways of perceiving reality you can both agree on.

Sometimes a conflict is created by the way you and your partner frame the situation. A "frame" is composed of the beliefs, thoughts, values, and assumptions with which you view the situation. Sometimes reframing the situation can open up new options or enable you to exercise personal capabilities that you've inhibited until now. A good reframe explains the facts as effectively as the old frame but permits new behaviors.

Reframe your life story as needed to create options and free up capabilities.

The most crucial frame of all is your life story. It tells you who you are and what is possible. But the life story you tell yourself is highly selective. Some of the experiences you leave out may tell a different story about who you are. Your present description of who you are and how you got here may be confining you. Look particularly at those parts of your life that don't fit easily into your normal life story. They may tell a different story.

Examine your self-talk to be sure it is serving you well, and reprogram it when you need to.

All of us have an inner voice that provides a running commentary on our life. Sometimes this commentary is negative: "Boy, that was a boneheaded thing to do," "Can't you do any better than that?" "You just don't know how to make friends, do you?" We often learn this kind of negative self-talk while growing up, from our parents or other significant adults. As children, we accepted these judgments as true. As adults, we need to examine negative self-talk that limits who we can be. More than that, we need to reprogram these negative thoughts.

Get to know the different parts of your personality and get them talking to each other.

We usually think of ourselves as a single, unified personality, even though different parts of our personality sometimes seem to be urging different courses of action. Most psychologists agree that we are all made up of a variety of subpersonalities. The part of you that gets locked in conflict with your partner may be only one of your subpersonalities; the others may perceive things differently and tell a different story. All the parts of your personality are trying to do something for you, but they may short-circuit each other or even fight over the best way to handle the situation. If you can identify these parts of yourself and get them into a conversation, they can learn from each other and agree on better strategies for taking care of you.

Accept that differences can make your relationships richer.

All couples have disagreements. The issue is how you handle them. It is true that when you normally feel very close, disagreement can create a feeling of separation. What's critical is whether you feel that you are working together to resolve the differences. The stronger the relationship, the more differences you can handle.

Live with the disagreement: engage it emotionally, don't gloss it over and pretend it has gone away.

Having used these approaches myself, I can predict one thing: if you and your partner commit to this path, your lives will be richer. Your differences will become teachers. You will grow together in ways that are both surprising and exciting.

When You Need Help

No matter how skilled a couple or how strong the bond of their relationship, periodically they are likely to encounter issues that turn their relationship into an emotional merry-go-round, going in circles with no apparent resolution in sight. When that happens, they may start looking outside their relationships for help.

Seeking Help from Friends

Many people turn to friends to discuss their problems. But while friends can offer great support in time of need, they can also reinforce many of the same attitudes and habits that triggered the problem in the first place. When couples are considering divorce, for example, it's not unusual for friends to side with one partner and freely criticize the other. Good friends are rarely neutral. They have a vested interest in our lives. If you want to resolve conflicts in your marriage, friends can't always give you what you need. You need someone who can step outside what is happening and bring fresh insights.

How can you tell if your friend can do this for you? Ask yourself the following questions. If your answer to more than two of them is yes, this friend may be important to you and a great source of support, but not neutral.

- Does the friend judge or evaluate your behavior or the behavior of the other person in the relationship?
- Does your friend tell you what you should do about your problem or feelings?
- Does your friend take sides?
- Does your friend have their own agenda for how you should act in the situation?

If this person is a close and trusted friend, you might still want to turn to them. You might want to discuss how the two of you can help each other in times of need by employing some of the skills we've discussed in this book. You might share what you've learned, or have them read the book, and practice some of the skills together. At the very least, you can make a pact with your friend to use active listening whenever either one of you requests help during a conflict. Your pact might include a promise to respect each other's need to make their own decisions, to be cautious about judging or evaluating the behavior of anyone else involved in the conflict, and to refrain from telling each other how to resolve problems.

Seeking Professional Help

If you can't rely on a friend to stay neutral, you may consider seeking professional help. Counselors and therapists are trained to stay neutral while helping you make decisions that hold true to your own values, needs, and interests. When they listen, they don't judge you. Instead, they listen in order to help you discover positive attitudes, feelings, and skills that you already have and can build on. They may also assist you in identifying beliefs and misunderstandings that might be blocking you from carrying out the solution that will work best for you.

Most therapists are careful about telling you what to do about your feelings. If they do advise you in a directive way, it would only be after getting to know you quite well. One of the goals of counseling and therapy is to help you strengthen your own abilities, not blindly follow your helper's advice.

A therapist is not a friend. In their private lives therapists have their own beliefs and feelings, their own friends, and their own conflicts. As professionals, their job is to help you focus on your thoughts and feelings and make the kinds of choices we've been describing throughout this book. The subject of every good counseling session is you — or your relationship, if you've come to therapy as a couple.

One of the great barriers to seeking outside help is that it involves admitting that there's a problem. Many people fear that seeking psychological help or counseling will automatically label them as sick, emotionally disturbed, or "really messed up." But modern-day counseling services increasingly focus on helping healthy people become more effective and happier in every area of their lives. Much counseling is now skill oriented — that is, aimed at helping people build their innate capacities for dealing with everyday life.

Many kinds of professional helpers are available in most communities. To help you choose the right one for you, here I list some of the categories of problems and the kinds of resources that are available to deal with them.

Skill Development

This book describes a number of skills that couples can use to resolve conflicts, including skills for listening, communicating feelings, and problem-solving. It's useful to gain some practice, in a safe, unthreatening setting, before trying to apply these skills in real life. Going through a training program as a couple is one way to create closeness as well as acquire skills.

Courses in communication skills are available through community colleges, mental health centers, parent-teacher organizations, and churches and other places of worship. Look for terms in the course descriptions such as *communications training, active listening, "I" messages, congruent sending,* and *win-win conflict resolution.*

You can also develop these skills by working with private counselors and consultants. My wife and I have gone to a therapist who helped us by allowing us to practice new skills while working on real-life issues, with the security that someone was there to help keep us on track if we became defensive or reactive.

Process, Relationship, and Personal Issues

When you are exploring options for resolving conflict, it can help to define the types of issues that are involved.

Process issues: Many of the factors leading to conflict have to do with the manner — the process — by which couples go about addressing issues, independent of the actual subject of the conflict. Because process is so often a matter of habit or so conditioned that we don't even think about it, couples sometimes need help seeing how the way they're trying to solve problems is setting them up for bitter fights. An objective person is often able to see process flaws in a way that the people who are deeply involved cannot. Sometimes these problems can be resolved quickly once both people see how the way they're relating is contributing to the problem.

Relationship issues: Conflicts in intimate relationships can bring up all kinds of issues: unresolved feelings about parents, intimacy, commitment, responsibility, unrealistic expectations — the list could go on and on. Even couples who are doing well with their "process" can still run into emotional issues that seem irresolvable. As two personalities interact to create a relationship, that relationship, like a third person, can take on aspects of both people's personalities. In relationship counseling, both people who helped create the relationship are present, and the focus is less on individual personality than it is on finding ways to make the relationship more satisfying.

Personal issues: You might seek counseling for personal issues because you feel inhibited in expressing your feelings, because you have unresolved anger or pain left over from your childhood, or because you are frequently depressed. All of these problems can put pressure on your relationship, turning them into relationship issues, and can even dictate how you cope with conflict. But they are still essentially your own personal issues and are best dealt with in that context.

In many cases you can talk with a prospective counselor over the phone before making a commitment to working with them. During the phone call (which will likely be limited to ten or fifteen minutes), or during your first counseling session, clearly describe what you want. Agree to work with the counselor only if you feel good about them. As in any professional relationship, personal trust is at least as important as credentials. So above all, honor your own feelings when picking a counselor.

Therapists and Counselors

The following are different kinds of therapists or counselors you might consider:

Marriage and family counselors: Therapists with training in marriage and family therapy are usually well qualified to deal with process and relationship issues. They may also have training and experience in teaching communication skills and working through process issues. Increasingly, marriage and family counselors are willing to help couples with short-term crises, that is, to help people address issues that are immediately pressing. In most states, marriage and family counselors are required to have credentials in social work, psychology, or marriage and family counseling.

Psychologists: Some psychologists are psychotherapists, and some are not. The type of psychologist who does therapy is usually identified as a clinical psychologist or psychotherapist. Some clinical psychologists work primarily on personal issues, while others are highly qualified to work on process and relationship issues as well. Tell any prospective psychologists what kinds of issues you want to work on, and feel free to ask about what kind of work they normally do.

Clinical social workers: Clinical social workers are normally trained in family therapy, as are marriage and family counselors; but they look not only at what's going on in the relationship, or even in the family, but also at how the broader community might be affecting or might provide resources to the couple. If relationship problems are compounded by problems such as substance abuse or domestic abuse, clinical social workers are well placed to recommend community resources that can be of help.

Psychoanalysts: Psychoanalysts do a form of in-depth therapy (analyzing dreams and events such as early childhood traumas) that can be extremely valuable for resolving personal issues. Psychoanalysis can involve a commitment to attend sessions at least once a week, or even daily, for several months or even years. As helpful as it may be in bringing insight and resolution to personal issues, it is not specifically designed to resolve process or relationship issues.

Religious and spiritual advisers: Couples may be more comfortable going to a spiritual adviser, such as a minister or rabbi, because they are confident that their adviser will share their own values. Many ministers and rabbis have received extensive training in pastoral counseling and are well qualified. But becoming a minister does not automatically mean that a person has trained as a counselor. If you are considering going to a spiritual adviser, ask about their training and experience and assess the degree to which counseling is one of their strengths. If you want to work on process or relationship issues, you'll want to ask if the person has a good background in addressing these topics.

Psychiatrists: Psychiatrists are medical doctors who specialize in mental health. A few are also psychoanalysts. As physicians, psychiatrists are the only counselors permitted to prescribe drugs. If you are dealing with a major emotional problem that can be managed with medication, then you will probably see a psychiatrist. Psychiatrists may also be helpful in addressing personal issues, but their ability to help with process or relationship issues depends on their interests and training outside their medical training in psychiatry. Some psychiatrists work in tandem with a psychotherapist. The psychiatrist prescribes drugs when necessary, and the psychotherapist works directly with the client on the emotional issues.

Mediators: If you are trying to resolve a major issue, and your primary emphasis is on getting it resolved rather than on gaining insights or relationship skills, you may want to consider a mediator. Mediators are increasingly used by family courts to resolve issues such as custody of children and financial support agreements. Mediation is also used to resolve landlord-tenant issues and even large community and environmental disputes. Essentially, mediators provide the "process" skills to help the various parties work together effectively to resolve their dispute. Mediators can structure meetings, guide the various participants, and teach communication skills to aid in problem-solving. Because a mediator's skills are primarily in the realm of process, few people use mediators to help resolve issues that are primarily emotional.

Not all therapists or counselors are trained in the specific therapeutic approaches described in this book. Here's where you can start looking for one who specializes in:

- **Transactional analysis:** United States of America Transactional Analysis Association, www.usataa.org/civicrm/?page=CiviCRM&q=civicrm/profile&gid=14
- **Family therapy:** The American Association for Marriage and Family Therapy, www.aamft.org/Directories/Find_a_Therapist.aspx
- **Internal family systems:** The Center for Self Leadership, https://selfleadership.org/find-an-ifs-therapist.html

There are significant differences in professional training among the specialties delineated above, but the differences between individuals in these professions may be even greater. As a result, you need to actually meet counselors and interview them before you make a commitment to work with them. The most important points are to know what kind of help you want and to specify this when you talk with prospective counselors. Feel free to ask about a counselor's background — don't be intimidated, just ask the questions you need to in order to be comfortable. Whether you feel comfortable with the counselor as a person and are convinced that they share enough of your values to be able to help you is quite possibly the most important criterion for selecting a helping professional.

In our busy lives, counselors and therapists are becoming more and more important. We can resolve important issues that might otherwise drag on for years. Counseling can provide access to knowledge and expertise that can vastly improve the quality of our relationships and the quality of our lives.

Acknowledgments

First I must acknowledge the contribution of my wife, Maggie Creighton. Everything in this book we lived together. My constant gratitude, Maggie, for the many years as a loving partner.

My sister, Florence Creighton, has been a therapist for many years. She was invaluable in every aspect of writing this book, reviewing drafts, recommending resources, and reassuring me that it was all worthwhile.

I gained valuable insights in this field from working with Dr. Thomas Gordon and Gene Merrill. Dr. Gordon spread the skills of active listening and "I" messages internationally with his parent effectiveness training, teacher effectiveness training, and leader effectiveness training. Mr. Merrill was my mentor and co-instructor for many years, and a dear friend. I also acknowledge the wise counsel of Dr. Thomas Parker, Dr. Russ Lee, and Dr. Ron Jones.

I am grateful for the many opportunities I had to explore new approaches to conflict resolution as a consultant to the U.S. Army Institute for Water Resources. I headed a team that helped create an award-winning alternative dispute-resolution program. I especially want to recognize the contribution of Dr. Jerome Delli Priscoli, the institute's program manager.

I knew Kimberley Cameron, my literary agent, when she was part of the Reece Halsey Agency team handling *Getting Well Again*. She now has her own successful agency. She doesn't ordinarily handle psychological self-help books, but she immediately bought into the concept of this book and promptly sold the book to exactly the right publisher. Great job, Kimberley.

Georgia Hughes, New World Library's editorial director, championed the book from the beginning. She's exactly what an author fantasizes about in an editor/publisher. It's a pleasure to work with a publisher whose principal goal is to publish books that change people's lives. I was very pleased with how often I was consulted during the production of the book. My thanks to everyone at New World Library, especially Kim Corbin, for her tireless efforts to publicize the book.

Notes

Chapter 2: Making Sense

Page 14, *William Crawford, a janitor at the US Air Force Academy*: James E. Moschgat, "Leadership and the Janitor," *On Patrol: The Magazine of the USO*, September 22, 2010, www.uso.org/stories/1758-leadership -and-the-janitor; "Medal of Honor Recipients: World War II (Recipients A–F)," United States Army Center of Military History, https://history .army.mil/moh/index.html, accessed July 16, 2018.

Page 19, *In a dramatic illustration of the Pygmalion effect*: Robert Rosenthal and Lenore Jacobson, *Pygmalion in the Classroom: Teacher Expectation and Pupils' Intellectual Development*, expanded ed. (New York: Irvington, 1992).

Chapter 3: Creating Reality

Page 25, *"Your control network…constantly shapes the course of your predictions"*: Lisa Feldman Barrett, *How Emotions Are Made: The Secret Life of the Brain* (New York: Houghton Mifflin, 2017), 154.

Chapter 5: Response-ability

Page 43, *When we learn response-ability*: Cartoon from "Conversational Reframing" by Mark Tyrrell, Uncommon Knowledge, used with permission, https://www.unk.com/blog/conversational-reframing -course.

Chapter 7: Listening

Page 60, *the pursuer/distancer dynamic*: See Gottman's description of this in his presentation "Making Relationships Work, Part 2," November 30, 2009, www.youtube.com/watch?v=-gFldZtVIqQ&t=6s, 2:35–4:10.

Page 61, *Gottman and his team observed fights between couples*: John M. Gottman, *The Marriage Clinic: A Scientifically Based Marital Therapy* (New York: W.W. Norton, 1999).

Page 67, *Active listening has been called by many different names*: The term *active listening* was originally coined by Carl Rogers and Richard Farson in *Active Listening*, a pamphlet published by the Industrial Relations Center, University of Chicago, 1957. See also "Active Listening," in *Communicating in Business Today*, ed. R. G. Newman, M. A. Danzinger, and M. Cohen (Lexington, MA: D.C. Heath, 1987). The concept and technique were popularized by Thomas E. Gordon. See his *Parent Effectiveness Training: The Proven Program for Raising Responsible Children* (New York: New American Library / Plume, 1975).

Chapter 8: Avoiding Escalation

Page 80, *In any relationship there are three parties*: I attribute this thought to the mythologist Joseph Campbell, but I've never been able to find the quote to prove it.

Chapter 11: Reframing

Page 103, *Mark Twain's fictional hero Tom Sawyer*: Mark Twain, *The Adventures of Tom Sawyer* (Chicago: American Publishing Company, 1876), chapter 2.

Page 105, *I remember a mini–paradigm shift*: Stephen Covey, *The Seven Habits of Highly Effective People* (New York: Free Press, 1989), 30–31.

Page 110, *"When someone is stuck in a particular thinking style"*: Mark Tyrrell, *New Ways of Seeing: The Art of Therapeutic Reframing* (Oban, Scotland: Uncommon Knowledge, 2014), xii, 22, 43–45.

Chapter 12: Reframing Your Life Story

Page 115, *"In any life there are always more events that don't get 'storied'"*: Jill Freedman and Gene Combs, *Narrative Therapy: The Social Construction of Preferred Realities* (New York: W.W. Norton, 1996), 32.

Chapter 14: Who Speaks for Your Internal Committee?

Page 141, *"distinct personalities, each with a full range of emotion and desire"*: Richard C. Schwartz, *Internal Family Systems Therapy* (New York: Guilford Press, 1995), 13.

Page 142, *Berne defined an ego state*: Eric Berne, *Transactional Analysis in Psychotherapy* (New York: Grove Press, 1961), 13.

Page 144, *Harris describes the adult*: Thomas Harris, *I'm OK, You're OK* (New York: Harper Perennial, 2004), 32–33.

Page 146, *Mehrabian shows that the listener focuses on three sources of information*: Albert Mehrabian, *Nonverbal Communication* (New York: Routledge, 2007).

Page 148, *"contain many different beings"*: Schwartz, *Internal Family Systems Therapy*, 9.

Page 148, *"Each of us 'contains multitudes'"*: Hal Stone and Sidra Stone, "Our Journey," Voice Dialogue International, delos-inc.com/index -intro.htm, accessed August 8, 2018.

Page 149, *"People are viewed as having all the resources they need"*: Schwartz, *Internal Family Systems Therapy*, 9.

Page 149, *"The human mind isn't a unitary thing"*: Jay Earley, *Self-Therapy: A Step-by-Step Guide to Creating Wholeness and Healing Your Inner Child Using IFS, a New, Cutting-Edge Psychotherapy* (Larkspur, CA: Pattern Systems Books, 2009), 3.

Page 149, *"Each part has a role to play in your life"*: Earley, *Self-Therapy*, 21.

Page 150, *"The critical or hurtful things that loved ones say about us"*: Schwartz, *Internal Family Systems Therapy*, 16.

Page 151, *Here are some techniques you can employ without a therapist*: See Earley, *Self-Therapy*.

Chapter 15: The Value of Being Different

Page 156, *"The fish will be the last to discover water"*: James C. Coleman, *Personality Dynamics and Effective Behavior* (Chicago: Scott, Foresman and Company, 1960), 59.

Index

acceptance, 62, 63, 69

accusation, 8, 79, 83, 158, 161. *See also* blame

active listening: in close relationships, 73–75, 76; defined, 33, 63; empathy behind, 59–60; examples, 65–66, 157–58; goal of, 63; guidelines for, 68–71; premise of, 69, 75; during problem-solving, 89; skills development for, 170; speaker as judge of, 71–72; typical listening vs., 67–68; use of term, 67; when to use, 72

adult ego state, 142–44, 145, 156

allies, claims of, 79–80, 82

American Association for Marriage and Family Therapy, 174

arguments, 3, 4. *See also* conflict

Asian Pacific cultures, 49

assumptions, 113, 163

attitudes: emotional reality created through, 4; friends and reinforcement of, 167; positive,

and professional help, 168–69; reframing and, 112, 113; self-talk and, 37, 128, 129, 130, 132–33, 137; social changes in, 16

balance, 99, 158

Barrett, Lisa Feldman, 25–26

behavior: beliefs and, 17, 21, 33; escalation-provoking, 8, 34, 75, 77–81, 83, 162; expectations as cue for other people's behavior, 20–21; family rules about, 47–48; family therapy and, 147, 148; gender differences in, 48; individual interpretations of, 4–5; judgments about, 69, 168; patterns of, and ego states, 140–41, 142–45; pursuer/distancer dynamic, 48, 60–62; reframing and, 9, 163; responsible communication and, 51, 56, 57; self-talk and, 36, 125, 128, 131, 132–33, 137; sense-making, 15; taking responsibility for, 81; values implied in, 100

183